# entwined

# entwined

## alex alberto

essays on polyamory
and creating home

QUILTED PRESS

**QUILTED PRESS**

info@quiltedpress.com
quiltedpress.com

This book depicts actual events in the author's life as truthfully as recollection permits and/or could be verified by research. All persons within are actual individuals; there are no composite characters. Dialogue has been reconstructed from memory. The names and identifying characteristics of some individuals or the events they took part in have been changed to respect their privacy. The author in no way represents any company, corporation, or band, mentioned in this book.

Excerpt from *The Family Outing: A Memoir* by Jessi Hempel. Copyright 2022 by Jessi Hempel. Published by HarperOne, San Francisco, CA.

Excerpt from *Real Queer America: LGBT Stories from Red States* by Samantha Allen. Copyright 2019 by Samantha Allen. Published by Bay Back Books, New York, NY.

Excerpt from *Heaven Is a Place on Earth: Searching for an American Utopia* by Adrian Shirk. Copyright 2022 by Adrian Shirk. Published by Counterpoint Press, Berkeley, CA.

A short passage of the essay *People Ask* was first published in HuffPost.

Cover design: Rachel Ake
Cover illustration: adapted from Shutterstock/bibadash
Interior Design: Alison Cnockaert

ISBN: 979-8-9896691-0-3 (paperback)
ISBN 979-8-9896691-2-7 (ebook)

# table of contents

# author's note

Dear reader,

Thank you for beginning *Entwined*. I'm thrilled that you're interested in my book. I've put years of work into it, and shared deeply personal details of my life and inner world in its pages. I know that there is an overabundance of content in the world, so I'm grateful that you're giving my story your attention. Regardless of your identity and approach to relationships—whether you're monogamous, polyamorous, aromantic, questioning—I sincerely hope that you receive something of value from reading about my experiences and emotions.

I wrote this book because, more than ten years ago, when I realized that monogamy was probably not for me, I craved narratives that showed various futures that could be available to me if I did the work of deprogramming *compulsory* monogamy. At the time, I didn't know what I could dream of. I needed stories that would give shape to my dreams, offer me hope, and not make me feel broken. I read many non-monogamy how-to and self-help books, but what I needed most was polyamorous versions of the millions of monogamous love stories that bombarded me from movies, books, TV, and the world that surrounded me.

What you're about to read is a collection of stories about my personal experiences, from the first naïve rumblings of desire for love "off script," to the seasoned polyamorous pleasures of bonding with a metamour (a partner's partner). In no way is this book meant to offer you advice, and it certainly isn't a how-to book. Ok, one essay is structured as a love advice column, but I used that form because it was a fun way to convey real life conversations I've had with friends and advice I gave them, as a *friend* who knows them and their specific situation. Instead of thinking of *Entwined* as a tool, I hope you'll be able to put yourself in my shoes—my heart, my body—and immerse yourself in my specific, personal journey. I also hope that reading this book stimulates an appetite for more polyamorous stories. There are millions in the world, and no two are alike.

**A note on the flavors of non-monogamy in *Entwined*.** Although I was single when I decided to pursue non-monogamy, I eventually developed a "primary partnership" with someone, and we operated under a tight hierarchical framework for a while. Throughout my essays, you'll see that relationship framework change, and watch me learn from some of the unethical behavior it gave rise to, as I do the work of deprogramming my own hierarchical notions of love. You may agree that my behavior was unethical, and you may not. There are innumerable ways to approach non-monogamy and structure relationships. I've defined for myself what I consider ethical and unethical, but I can't do that for you.

So, yes, there is suffering in this book. But at its core, *Entwined* is a happy story. There are struggles, but probably no more than you see monogamous couples navigate in popular narratives. I've tried to give you a nuanced portrait of who I am, and who my partners and the other people in these pages are. We are human. All of us are flawed, none are irredeemable, and everyone in this book is still learning and growing.

**A note on essay form and order.** I approached writing these essays the same way I now approach relationships: I allow each one to become what it wants to be without pushing it into a predefined box. Some essays are creative and nontraditional in form. There is a play, a triptych, a love letter, but they're all my story. Also, I chose the order in which the essays are presented because I think it's the order that makes the overall narrative easiest to grasp, but each essay can be read in isolation. Read them in any order you like.

**A note on my pronouns.** In some essays, I chose to show the pronouns I used at the time those events happened. In others, I updated them to reflect the ones I use today. At the time of publication, I use they/them pronouns, but I'm still on my gender journey and my gender is fluid. I show that fluidity in the book. I describe my thinking and experiences with gender in the essay *Queer en français*. If understanding my gender is important for you to settle into the narrative, you're welcome to begin there.

## author's note

**A note on my process and memory.** This book is a collection of essays that are true. I've gone to great lengths to record as much of my non-monogamy journey as possible in real-time. My partners have been incredibly gracious to allow me to record some conversations we had (especially the difficult conversations), I kept an electronic journal with date/time stamps, I've cataloged emails, text messages, and voice notes with a degree of obsessiveness that is natural to me (and odd to others). Still, my records could not capture every important detail of this story, and human memory is fallible. I've focused on truth as much as I could throughout this book, but it's *my* truth. Every story has a point of view. This is mine.

There are specific aspects of the book that are not technically "true." Some names and identifying characteristics have been changed to preserve the privacy of characters who either requested de-identification or were not contacted. Their behaviors and dialogue are faithfully represented, but I tried my best to make it difficult for a general reader to be able to determine the identity of the individual(s) portrayed.

**Notes on content.** This book contains some descriptions of consensual sex—a few include BDSM (whipping, bondage, etc.), sometimes with anatomically correct terms. Also, because I am a nonbinary, polyamorous, queer person writing a true story, I describe instances of homophobia, biphobia, transphobia, and monogamy-centric viewpoints. Death, loss and illness have been a part of my life, so you will encounter mentions of health-related PTSD, drowning, and a car accident, as well as descriptions of a stroke, parental loss, and family dysfunction. These kinds of experiences are important for fully comprehending my story, and they make the joy and curiosity that define it that much sweeter.

**How to connect with me.** I *love* to hear about ways that readers relate to my writing, and what it means to them. You can send emails to hello@alexalberto.com. You can also find me on Instagram and TikTok @thatalexalberto. My website is alexalberto. com. Sign up for my newsletter if you want to hear about my upcoming events and future work.

And if you want to read (or hear) more stories of nontraditional love, friendship, and family, subscribe to *Entwined Mag* at entwinedmag.com. You'll receive monthly stories in your inbox.

Thank you again for going on this journey with me. I hope that you find it even half as fun and engrossing to read as it did to write.

# entwined

# a glossary of love(s)

## Friends-with-Benefits | 2009-2010

Sometimes, while my former roommate Matt was out on a date, I'd lay on top of his cream duvet wearing black lacy thigh highs and a sheer top and read a fantasy romance novel. Then he'd come home, climb on top of me, and I'd unbutton his linen shirt and ask how her lips felt, what she smelled like. Or, I'd tell him about the towering jazz musician I tied up in a hotel room and whipped with his own brown belt, or about the woman in my teaching program who wore a leather coat and Doc Martens, and how I fantasized about undressing her in a single-stalled bathroom after class.

And often he'd cook me pesto fusilli with fresh cherry tomatoes, then I'd wash our dishes, and we'd sink into his faded green couch and massage each other's feet in front of *How I Met Your Mother*.

## Relationship Escalator | 2010-2012

When I was in college in Montreal, I unexpectedly hooked up with my classmate Daniel. The morning after, I woke up in his bed, nestled in his arms, my cheek resting on his delightfully hairy chest. *I'd like to do this again*, I told him in his entryway while sliding my winter boots on. *But I just broke up with someone and I don't want anything serious.* Code for non-exclusive. He agreed.

When he spent two months teaching abroad, I counted the days until he would be back. I felt a certain kind of full-body flutters for Daniel that I didn't experience with my best-friend-with-benefits. I figured this meant I loved-loved Daniel, and that meant we should be exclusive.

He cleared a drawer for me in his bedroom, the second one from the top, the one between his white briefs and his colorful t-shirts.

I moved in with him, and we spent our weekends doing DIY projects like painting a bird mural in the kitchen and building metallic light fixtures for the red-walled living room.

We received our education degrees and moved from Montreal to a remote village in Nova Scotia to teach at the same school. We sat in staff meetings together, crammed around a small table, our knees touching.

*Having a kid might be nice, no?* Daniel told me one night while I was rummaging through the fridge in search of leftover tomato paste. *I can't imagine myself with a kid*, I said, scooping the paste out of the can and dropping it into the chili pot.

I didn't want to get married.

"Forever" didn't sound romantic to me, it sounded claustrophobic.

## One Penis Policy | 2013

In the car on our way to school, I told Daniel I'd developed a crush on one of our coworkers, a jaunty brunette with a charming Acadian accent. I squeezed the wheel and glanced at the Bay to my left. The windy road followed the coast, and the November rain created a thin layer of fog over the silver-blue water. Every morning, even on gray days, I took a moment to savor this landscape and the fortune I had to live in this breathtaking part of the Maritimes. But Daniel and I lived together, worked together, drove weekly for forty-five minutes to the nearest grocery store together, and shared all the same friends—other teachers at our school. I told him I wanted to try an open relationship. I often initiated difficult conversations in the car. Something about the obligation to stare forward made me feel more courageous.

3

"Okay," he said, unsure. "But you can only sleep with women."

He thought my only two needs could be *penis* and *vagina*. I didn't think to ask how he'd feel if I hooked up with a man who didn't have a penis, or a woman who did. I had yet to unearth my own repressed gender-queerness. I didn't even think to ask how he'd feel if I spent time with someone I didn't have sex with, but who would hold my hand, spoon me, and send me long heartfelt emails. I figured that *women only* was the best deal I could get. As we passed the green wooden siding of La Cuisine Robicheau, the best seafood restaurant on the coast, I told Daniel he could sleep with other women too—or men, if he ever wanted to—but he didn't seem particularly interested. Over the three years we'd been together, I'd patiently broken through his wall of dry humor and stoicism. I knew he was too self-conscious and guarded to put himself out there like that.

When we went to Montreal the following month for the holiday break, I started sleeping with a middle school friend who didn't consider sleeping with other women as cheating on her boyfriend. I saw her every time I visited.

The next spring, on the three-hour car ride from our home to the Halifax airport, I told Daniel I didn't want to be limited to women—but didn't confess that I'd already been sleeping with a man, my ex-best-friend-with-benefits whom I was still close to.

"If you want to sleep with other dudes," he said, raising his voice "then you don't love me anymore." He'd never yelled at me before.

"Non, je t'aime encore!" I said, the words muffled by my tears and the rumble of 18-wheelers speeding past.

It was true. I did still love him.

"We need to break up," he replied.

I cried on and off through security. Sitting at the gate. On the plane, shoving pretzels into my mouth, chewing them into a pasty ball that I struggled to swallow. When I tried to hold Daniel's hand, he pulled his forearm off the armrest in between our seats.

I spent that summer crying daily on my commute, resting my head on the steering wheel at red lights, wondering why I couldn't be happy with monogamy, like everybody else.

## The Lifestyle | 2013

When I moved from Nova Scotia to New York City for grad school, I was adamant that I needed a combination of friends-with-benefits and committed partnerships. I needed a relationship framework that kept me free and my own whole person. But I didn't know where to look for people interested in non-monogamy. I'd never tried online dating, but I was certainly not going to broadcast my shameful proclivities on "mainstream" apps.

I sat on the beige futon against the brick wall in my Brooklyn studio and set my after-work glass of wine on the side table. On my laptop, I typed keywords into Google like *alternative dating* and *non-monogamous dating*. I found websites with terrible names like swinglifestyle.com that were designed in the nineties and had not been updated since. When I thought of swingers, I imagined spray-tanned white people in their sixties going to key parties in New Jersey. I couldn't possibly be the only person in my twenties looking for an open romance. *We have helped millions of people find traditional partners, swinger groups, threesomes, and a variety of other alternative partners*, one site said. The futon squeaked as I downed my glass of wine, set it on the table loudly, and clicked *Sign Up*.

The next evening, I logged into my account to rummage through my overflowing inbox. I propped my pillows on the wall behind my lofted bed and sat up. I opened a message from a guy named Jay. Jay was a 29-year-old bulky sales guy with a tribal tattoo on his left pec. *How long have u been in The Lifestyle?* Jay wrote. This was often the first question people asked (or the second, right after *Are you real?*).

Commonly found on profiles: *Fit, DDF* (drugs and disease-free, Google taught me), *can host, no-drama*, and *I can share face pics once we connect*.

While I didn't want *just* sex, I was coming out of a monogamous relationship. I was twenty-four years old, and I'd just moved to a city that had as many people as my entire home province of Québec. I was on a self-discovery quest, and I was hungry for corporeal exploration. I deleted Jay's message and moved to the next one.

## Don't Ask, Don't Tell | 2014

Carlos had an arrangement with his girlfriend: They were allowed to see other people, as long as they did it covertly. They left no trace of their affairs, and pretended their other lovers didn't exist. I wasn't thrilled with that, but I'd been living in New York for six months and Carlos was the first person I'd met who was attractive and wrote in complete sentences. His lips were plump and sweet, he kissed me deeply but not messily, and our bodies nested into one another perfectly. We spent hours having acrobatic sex against my studio window, in the spiral staircase that led to the lofted bed, and on my kitchen floor, nudged between the refrigerator and oven.

One late afternoon, I sat at my desk in front of my one window, which overlooked the sidewalk, secured by thick bars. The last rays of spring sun reflected on the grooved bark of the naked Ash tree across the street. I opened my text thread with Carlos. He had not replied to my last three messages, and I had not seen him for three weeks. I pressed the spacebar on my laptop to shake it out of sleep mode and pulled up my swinglifestyle.com profile. I typed a new line: *I'm not interested in Don't Ask Don't Tell arrangements. If you have a partner, I want to meet them at least once.* I clicked on the inbox tab. Some dude had sent me a message: *hi gorgeous. how long u been in the lifestyle?* I sighed, but then noticed the first buds of the season on the branches of the Ash tree.

## Unicorn | 2014

A few weeks after Carlos vanished, I met a tattooed insurance agent named Rosa, and her boyfriend Steve, a short, bulky construction worker with a square jaw. They drove in from South Jersey for our date. People traveled long distances for the elusive single femme willing to meet with a couple. In fact, I had started to wonder if I was the only one—I hadn't been able to connect with *any* single woman on my dating websites. Rosa suggested we meet at Madame X in Greenwich Village.

I descended the carpeted staircase and sat on a red velvet couch behind a round cocktail table. I was vibrating with anticipation; nervous to meet a couple for the first time, but looking forward to the exploration. The decor was meant to be vintage and sultry, with red lightbulbs in the sconces that hung on the brick wall, and red curtains. Almost every couch: red. There was an off-putting smell of artificial smoke.

Rosa walked in wearing a tight pencil dress under an unbuttoned green felt coat. I tuned out the electro jazz music and the lights momentarily brightened. She was fit and compact, with the curvy black lines of a thigh tattoo peeking out below the hem of her dress and through her sheer tights. I almost missed Steve behind her. Rosa sat on the couch next to me and Steve asked what I wanted to drink. "Rye whiskey, neat," I said, my go-to choice when wanting to seem sexy and serious.

When he returned, Steve handed me my drink and sat on the opposite side of Rosa. I realized that put me at ease, to be closer to her first. I liked that she was the driving force and that Steve was more laid back. She was bubbly and touched my thigh to punctuate her stories. Steve was quiet. Attractive in a brooding sort of way. We discussed our motivations for creating profiles on *SLS*, the only thing we seemed to have in common, though it felt like an important one. I rarely got to connect openly about my wants and desires, especially with a woman. I liked how confident and shameless Rosa was. I found it inspiring.

They rented a hotel room near the bar. We didn't want to trek to my apartment in Brooklyn, plus I didn't see how the three of us could climb into my lofted bed, which had only three feet of ceiling space. The hotel room was fancier than I expected, on the thirty-second floor, with a modern soaking tub next to the king-sized bed. The implicit rule was that the couple should pay for everything. *They* were taking *me*—the rare unicorn—out. I lavished the attention and spoiling.

I saw Rosa and Steve a few times, then Jess and Daryl, then Ben and Rhea. I loved being the center of attention, part of a couple's fantasy. But after a few meetings, it usually became clear that was all I was: a fantasy. I wanted something deeper. I wanted the three of us to cuddle and binge true crime shows. Go to the Museum of Natural History and publicly hold hands. Spend a weekend camping together in the Catskills and play Rummy by the fire. Typically, after dinner on the first date, the couples wanted sex to be our main—and *only*—activity.

The world was designed for pairs, so I began to think maybe it would be easier to look for what *they* had. After all, I had never seen any model of a successful three-way relationship. All I'd absorbed from popular culture was that wild couples might have sex with a third; not that they would ever care for the third the way they did each other.

## Primary Partner | 2015

I lay in my lofted sleeping nook wearing cotton mini shorts. A small fan clipped to the pipe above me blew air on my body. I always found it hard to fall asleep on Sunday evenings, and that September was unusually hot and humid. I combed through the row of tiny pictures in my OkCupid inbox, holding my phone above my face. Since "alternative" websites had yielded only couples who were uninterested in meaningful relationships and dudes who thought that *non-monogamy* meant *casual side piece*, I decided to ask for what I wanted on a "normal" dating app. Though I still cropped my pictures below my eyes, in case people from my new startup job came across my profile.

A beard and blue eyes caught my attention. I loved hairy men.

Don's OkCupid profile was well written, a rarity. He was a psychologist, so I assumed he was emotionally literate—another rarity.

In a dark semi-basement wine bar the next day, I asked Don about his work. *I research how our minds can sometimes break our hearts*, his profile said.

"I follow survivors of acute life-threatening medical events, primarily heart attacks," he said, and put his glass of Lambrusco down, "and measure their levels of psychological distress. What we've found is that they develop something that looks like PTSD. But contrary to PTSD from combat or assault, the threat remains *inside* their body." He uncrossed his legs, touched his sternum with one hand, fingers spread. His eyes looked small, between his tall forehead and long straight nose. But there was a captivating intensity to them. His blinking slowed and his eyes grew.

"They can't escape that threat. They can't lock the doors or remind themselves they're not at war anymore. So they become hyper attuned to bodily signals that most of us ignore. Like our pulse racing or the occasional short breath. And the patients who develop PTSD are more likely to have another heart attack."

"What made you interested in researching this?" I asked, and pushed my small fork through a spicy olive in our shared bowl.

"Well, I sort of landed into it by accident during my postdoc. But now, I'm waiting on funding to start a similar project with stroke survivors."

My back straightened. I put my fork down and felt my pulse in my wrist.

"All research is *mesearch* in psychology," he said. "When I was a teenager, my grandfather—Granddaddy—had a stroke. Of all the people that made up my world as a young person, he seemed to me the most indestructible. He was the most powerful. But one day, he became immobile and incomprehensible. It altered my sense of what it meant to be safe in the world."

"What do you mean, incomprehensible?" I asked, looking at my wine glass in my hand.

"The only word he could say was *damn*. He repeated it all day. *Damn damn damn damn damn.* Though one day we learned that he could sing happy birthday if we began the song for him. And it made him happy."

I nodded and smiled faintly. Don leaned in, and I felt warm under his gaze. I sensed him reading me.

"Do you know much about strokes?" he asked.

"I... I do. Yeah. My dad had one five years ago. I'm just... I'm floored because we've never seen anyone else have it as bad as him. His whole right side is paralyzed, and he can't speak. The whole time he was in rehab, patients either had aphasia, or paralysis. Never both."

Don laid his hand on the back of mine. He wrapped his fingers around my palm.

"I'm so sorry," he said.

I didn't usually let a first date hold my hand. It felt more intimate than kissing. Once, someone reached for my hand and I pulled it back as soon as our skin touched, as if I'd been burned. Don's hand soothed me.

"I wish you didn't have dinner plans," Don said after we got the check. "I'd take you for a stroll." The wine made his southern accent thicker—and sexier. "Are you getting together with friends?"

I hesitated. But I'd promised myself I'd be fully honest with any prospective partner. And I really, *really* liked Don. "I'm actually spending the night at someone's place..." I said. His eyebrows twitched. "A woman I've been seeing for a few weeks. She lives around here."

"Alright," he said, his flicker of discomfort contained. "Do you want me to walk you there?"

"That would be nice," I said, pleasantly surprised.

We walked up Amsterdam in the warm fall breeze and stopped in front of the massive Cathedral St. John the Divine, its dozens of sharp peaks and hand carved statuettes looking down on us. We stood at the bottom of the imposing stone steps.

Don turned to face me. "I love this church," he said. "It's beautiful, even if technically it's unfinished. It was originally designed in a Romanesque style, but somewhere during the construction, they changed it to this Gothic Revival style."

"How do you know this?" I asked Don, not so subtly stepping closer to him.

"I studied history and religion in my undergrad," he said. "The architecture of churches fascinates me."

I nodded with a closed smile, holding his gaze. He bent down and pressed his lips on mine. Our kiss was warm and deep, as natural as it was to hold hands.

The next day, Don and I made plans for a second date.

The woman I was seeing moved to Seattle for work, so my fling with her was short-lived. Within a few months, my life and Don's were woven together: I joined him on a work retreat in the mountains with his coworkers, we ate eggs in in our underwear every Saturday morning, he met my mother over tea during one of her visits, he read aloud to me in bed at night and knew the exact moment I fell asleep based on the sound of my breathing. We began reading books about non-monogamy, but promised that we would always come first for each other.

## Veto Power | 2016

I sat on the couch next to Don, jiggling my left heel on the living room rug, causing the leg crossed over my knee to shake in the air. I watched Don scroll through my WhatsApp message thread with Lukas, an Austrian guy I'd gone on a few dates with when he'd traveled to New York. Don took loud drags of his e-cigarette. I looked up at the sconce on the wall, a light sculpture made by Don's friend. Tiny crystal shapes were assembled in two elongated clusters, one floating above the other, projecting wide geometric patterns onto the white wall. The sculpture was titled *Billowy #1*, and according to his friend, played with the idea of attraction vs. repulsion.

Don tossed my phone on the cushion between us. "I don't think I'll ever feel comfortable with you dating him," he said. He leaned back and crossed his arms, speaking in a measured, resolved tone. "It's best to just move on from that and start fresh with someone else."

Lukas was the first person I'd dated since meeting Don five months prior. I didn't yet understand how unethical it was to let Don read my text messages. But according to the couples we met at polyamorous meetups, it was standard practice.

"You took too long to tell him about me," Don said, "and you live in the same building. He can show up at your door or on the rooftop any time, and I have no control over when that can happen."

"Well," I replied, "he doesn't live in the building, his cousin does. And he's not even in New York often."

Don cocked his head. "Still."

I was gutted at the idea of ending things with Lukas before they'd begun. It was so rare I met someone I was really into, and even rarer to meet them in the analog world. But I wanted to be able to exert the same power over Don, should he meet someone who threatened the established hierarchy I sat atop—or who just made me feel insecure.

Don took a long drag on his e-cigarette, looking into my eyes. He exhaled, his mouth twisted to blow the smoke to the side. We sat in silence for a few seconds or minutes. I scraped under the nail of my left middle finger with my right thumb.

"How hard will it be to run into him in the hallway and stay away?" Don asked, his voice gentler this time.

"Oh, don't worry about that, you can trust me."

"I know I can," he said. His jaw loosened. "I'm asking if it will cause you pain to stay away because I asked you to."

I searched in his eyes, trying to decipher the intention behind his question. "It's hard to ignore the intensity of the feelings I have for him," I replied honestly.

He took a slow breath in and out of his nose, keeping his lips shut.

"Well, we didn't set out to do non-monogamy only when it doesn't matter," he deliberated. "You should see him when he comes. But I want to meet him."

I felt relief and joy, but as my eyes followed the sharp edges of the light sculpture, my gut twisted. Would Lukas be willing to meet with Don? How hard would it be to manage Don's emotions *and* Lukas's needs?

## New Relationship Energy, or NRE | 2016

During my first few months with Lukas, I felt energized by our bond. I counted the weeks and days until he'd visit New York. I thought about him as I fell asleep, and checked my texts as soon as I woke up, hoping he'd sent one when he'd woken up six hours earlier, in his time zone. He did, every day.

I felt as if I had unlocked a secret level in a video game and discovered new superpowers: Simultaneously experiencing love with Don that rested on a solid foundation and long-term commitment, and the emotional and physical rush that came with my new infatuation with Lukas.

## Compersion | 2016

For our second New Year's Eve together, Don hosted a gathering at his apartment in Morningside Heights. It was bitterly cold out, and snow was accumulating. Among the guests were Bridget, who he'd been dating for eight months, and her primary partner. I sat on the beige couch in the corner, and Bridget sat on a chair on the other side of the boomerang-shaped coffee table. Don came back from the kitchen with a tall glass of sparkling water filled almost to the brim. He walked lighter than usual, graceful even. Don wore black t-shirts and jeans almost every day, but tonight he wore a striped button down and left his collar opened.

Our friends were cozily scattered around the room, on the couch, on folding chairs, on the rug, laughing and sipping on their wine tumblers. Don stood behind Bridget, rested his hand on her shoulder. She was wearing a sleeveless dress that accentuated her muscular arms and her square shoulders. She still had a dancer's body and her posture had a straightness, a power to it. Don slowly lowered the glass in front of her. She took it and looked up behind her shoulder. Don moved his hand to her back and rested it under her long, ruby red hair. They looked at each other for a few moments, and I saw tenderness, intimacy, and passion. It was their first New Year's Eve together.

Multiple conversations were happening around the room, the jazzy holiday music was loud over the thrum of cars on the West Side Highway out the window. But everything surrounding Don and Bridget dimmed. At that moment, I felt the opposite of jealousy. I felt a swell of happiness for him, and for being able to witness a glimpse of their love. I was delighted that Don had found someone else to share a part of his life with. Someone who made him happy in a different way than I did. My lung capacity momentarily expanded; I breathed in a crisp air that made me lighter.

## Nesting Partner, Anchor Partner | 2017

I poured blue shower gel in circular motion onto Don's luffa and put the bottle back on the corner of the tub. I stood under the shower head with Don in front of me. I squeezed the tan spongy material like Don liked, making it extra foamy. Hot water ran down my back. I soaped Don's hairy chest, then his svelte thighs.

"How about *nesting partner*?" Don asked. A year into our relationship, Don and I began to shift away from the hierarchical framework of *primary* and *secondary partners*. We were looking for new terms to describe each other.

"I've heard it before," I said, carefully running the luffa on his groin. "But people use it to say they live together. Technically we don't."

Don turned, and I washed the tattoo of Sisyphus surrounded by clouds that covered his arm and shoulder. I always liked that tattoo, a testament to Don's affinity for existentialist philosophy. In Greek Mythology, Sisyphus, punished by Hades, was forced to roll a boulder up a hill, and every time he reached the top, the immense rock rolled back to the bottom. Sisyphus pushed it up again and again, for eternity.

"I saw *anchor partner* somewhere the other day," I said, turning the shower knob to lower the temperature before Don took my place directly under the showerhead. He picked up the soap bar and ran it across my back. I shivered.

"I like that one," he said.

"Yeah," I added. "And I guess in the future we could have multiple anchors."

I wasn't ready to drop all qualifiers to *partner* yet.

## Kitchen Table Polyamory | 2018

"For us, metamours are like in-laws," Don told Frank and Gabriela as he laid out the hexagon Catan tiles for ore, brick, lumber, grain, and wool across the table. "You should get to know them, see them at least every once in a while, and pay them respect. And if you actually like them and want to develop a deeper friendship with them, great. It makes for a happier situation, but it's not necessary."

I'd been seeing Frank for two months, and it was the second time we got together with him and his wife. We were thrilled when we'd learned that Frank and Gabriela liked board games. We'd been having a hard time finding game partners. Frank carefully piled his orange road, settlement, and city wooden pieces, creating a sculpture. I welled up in affection. Frank always kept his hands busy with whatever he could find on a table.

"It's a deal-breaker for me now," I said, shuffling the resource cards. "When someone tells me they refuse to meet my partners or hangout like this."

"Maybe we can rename this *board game polyamory*," Frank said. We all laughed.

"*Love* it," Don said, and placed the Robber pawn on the desert tile.

## Metamour | 2019

Don stood in my narrow living room in front of the bookcase I'd built out of planks and cinder blocks and secured his helmet.

It looked out of place on his head, and he seemed much taller than 6'2" next to his new folding bike with small wheels. Something about this image of him was both endearing and comical. I stood from the couch and raised my phone to take a picture of him, then sat back down and scrolled to my text thread with Bridget. But my thumb froze above the send button. I didn't know the norms for interacting with an ex-metamour. I knew that Don and Bridget were taking a break from communicating, but did that mean I should refrain from reaching out? Their breakup was amicable, but Don missed her. Maybe a picture of him would make her smile—but what if it had the opposite effect?

"I'll be back soon," Don said on his way out, holding the door open with his back to push his bike out. "Je t'aime!"

"Bye, je t'aime," I replied without looking up from my phone.

Before exploring non-monogamy, I hadn't thought about what a relationship with a metamour might bring to my life. Over the two years Bridget and Don had dated, I discovered an unexpected new joy: exchanging endearing pictures of a mutual partner. Like when Don's mother sent me pictures of a 1995 photoshoot for his high school graduation. In one, 16-year-old Don wore a taupe turtleneck. He lay on his side in front of a shiny silver backdrop, looking at the camera with something between seductive and serial killer eyes, his mouth awkwardly shut to hide his braces. In another, he held the temple tip of his glasses to his mouth like a slutty librarian in a cheesy porno. When I shared those pictures with Bridget, we laughed so hard our jaws ached. The kind of laughing *at* someone that's infused with love and endearment, and that you can only experience when you truly love them romantically. I'd never shared that feeling with anyone.

I walked to the patio door and pulled the screen open, looking out at my tiny walled backyard, with the beautiful perennial garden that Bridget had helped me start in the spring. The ferns looked lush and happy, tripled in size under the shade of my neighbor's maple tree, but my boxwood bushes were patchy and I wasn't sure how to help them. I loved Bridget in a way I didn't know existed before; a mix of friendship, fondness, intimacy, and trust that stemmed from our romantic love for the same human.

I closed the screen door and looked at my phone again. I stared at the picture of Don and his bike, chuckling at his white socks pulled up mid-calf. I erased my text.

## Poly-Saturated | 2020

"You're wearing *men's* boxers!" Cara said after she pulled my jeans down. "This is so sexy." She tugged at my fly. I laid down onto the kitchen floor on my back, and she kneeled between my legs. I pulled her tightly against me, my hand pressed in the hollow of her lower back. It was my favorite way to hold her, anchoring me in the heart of her soft curves. Out of the house, she wore loose clothing. Cotton or wool items naturally dyed in earth tones. But in private, she showed off her hourglass figure with tight leggings and tees. I couldn't keep my hands off of her.

I'd been seeing Cara for a few months. On that cold December afternoon, we embraced on couch cushions spread across the checkered kitchen floor, in front of the wood stove. This had become part of our ritual: We'd take a walk in the snow, then return to the cabin I'd rented for the winter, make tea, add a log to the fire, and peel the layers off one another. It made me feel whole to see her aroused by the masculine parts of me.

"I like your thick thighs," she said, running her hand up my leg, "and how you look in this flannel." She unbuttoned my collar, then brushed her fingers behind my ear, sending shivers down to my belly button. "And I *love* your short hair."

I was five years into my relationship with Don. I spent Sundays and Mondays upstate with Cara, Tuesdays and Wednesdays alone, and Thursdays, Fridays and Saturdays with Don. He'd either come Upstate to my cabin, or I'd drive down to the city to see him.

I liked how Don made me feel little, cared for, held. I liked how Cara made me feel big, strong, masculine. Never had I felt more balanced and complete.

When I connected with Cara on Lex, a queer app, she told me that she had never been in a polyamorous relationship, but she'd been curious about it for a long time. I preferred dating poly-experienced people who knew their needs and boundaries, but after just one call, my connection to her was strong.

I lay on my side behind Cara, spooning her in front of the stove. I felt the warmth of the fire on my cheeks. In between kisses on her neck, I told Cara I was surprised that she hadn't yet had poly struggles.

"I think it's because Don was already in your life when I met you," she replied, and rolled on her back towards me. "But it's been on my mind that it would be hard for me if you met someone new now."

I kissed her forehead, pushed myself up to a seat, and stretched my arm to reach my steamy mug sitting on the counter behind me.

"That makes sense," I said, and took a careful sip. I rested my hand on her stomach, and she put both hers on top of it. "But I feel pretty saturated with two partners right now. If I organically met someone that I was drawn to, it would have to become something that orbits pretty loosely around my life."

She took a long breath in, her stomach pressing against our hands, and exhaled. She nodded. Did I perceive relief? I wondered if I'd regret my answer someday. What if my future included a lover I'd want to integrate deeply into my life? But it was how I truly felt in that moment: filled to the brim.

## Triad | 2021

Six years into my relationship with Don, and two years into his relationship with his partner Aly, Aly broke up with her nesting partner. Aly and I had developed a strong friendship. I'd recently broken up with Cara, so I had space and energy to step up and give Aly the support she needed.

We went apartment hunting to find her a home close to the one Don and I shared in the city. She stood inside one ground floor apartment on the quiet side street while I stood outside, the fall wind blowing leaves on the sidewalk, and lifted the garbage container cover to slam it shut a few times. We were trying to assess the volume of noise careless neighbors might make just outside her window. It was too much, and too depressing to have a view over the building's trash.

When she worked long days at her office down in the Financial District, I walked Casino, her fluffy Black Lab and Golden Retriever mix, in Riverside Park. Casino would drag me all the way to the dog park, pulling on the leash with uncontainable excitement, tongue flapping out one side. When a dog owner complimented me on Casino's shiny coat and asked me how old she was, I thanked them and said *almost two years old*, pretending she was mine, bending down to pat her head.

Over Mexican takeout, Aly and I talked about buying a car that she, Don, and I could share. We dreamed about building a new cabin on the farmland Don and I had just purchased Upstate with a friend. A small home with a writing nook, a sleeping loft, and space for her cats—Don and I are allergic.

Aly, Don, and I spent more and more time together. We had four-way cuddling sessions on the couch, Aly sitting between Don and me, her head on Don's shoulder, my arm wrapped around, Aly's hand on my thigh, Don's arm stretched over Aly to reach my neck with his hand, and Casino spread across all of our laps, eyes half-closed, almost smiling.

## Polycule, Constellation, Chosen Family— or why not *Family*? | 2023

I've never seen myself in a traditional nuclear family. I wanted something just as loving and enduring, but more intentional and creative. A family that would allow me to grow and embody all the different parts of me. Bridget and Aly taught me that poly-amory could help me develop that kind of family.

My polycule—the network of my partners and their partners—is a web of beautiful relationships; the lines between partners, friends, companions, and lovers are blurred, and we get to design, negotiate (and renegotiate) terms of each relationship as we grow and evolve together.

Sometimes I wish I could introduce anyone who's part of my polycule as my *family*. "Hi, this is Arielle, a member of my family." But when I do, I often see confusion on people's faces. They ask how we are related. If I introduce someone as my *metamour*, or my *partner's partner*, they are doubly puzzled. And if I intro-duce someone as my *partner*, it's assumed they're my *only* partner. So now I say *one of my partners*, and ignore the question mark-shaped eyebrows as best I can.

I don't like the word *polycule*. It's the most widely recognized in polyamorous circles, but to me, it sounds like a disease. Some-thing you get surgically removed or burnt off your skin.

I much prefer *constellation*. I like to see my loved ones as a group of stars of various distance and luminosity, connected to-gether by threads of meaning. Bonds that are no less powerful for being invisible to nature. My constellation guides me, gives my life structure and purpose.

A family.

# hierarchy as heartbreaker

I sat on a folding chair on my building rooftop, working from home on a Friday morning, when two sparkly blue eyes appeared above my laptop. I pulled my noise canceling headphones down and Lukas said hello with a wide smile. My brain flooded. He lived in Vienna and crashed at his cousin's place two floors above mine when he traveled to New York for work. I seemed to be the only tenant who enjoyed the rooftop; the access was up a ladder through a hatch and there were only three half broken lawn chairs scattered on the uneven tarred roof surface. But I'd bumped into Lukas twice during his last visit a few months prior. Like me, he seemed to enjoy outdoor computer work, even on this crisp fall day. I'm not sure what I said to him before he sat down in the shaded corner by the chimney and popped his headphones in. I grabbed my phone and texted Don.

> Remember that super cute and charming guy
> from Vienna who stays in my building when

he's in town? He's back! When I saw him, my
heart started pounding, and my palms got
sweaty just from talking to him.

I remember, Don replied. You have to ask him out!

This was the moment Don and I had been preparing for since our first date, three months prior. During that date, I'd explained to Don that my interest in non-monogamy was not about volume; I found online dating exhausting and didn't expect to constantly meet new people.

"No matter how great any relationship might be," I'd said, "it's fundamentally important to me to feel free. I don't want to have to choose between my current partner and the *idea* of everyone else. And I don't want any individual partner of mine to feel pressured to be everything to me."

I mentioned my neighbor's cousin as an example.

"Nothing has happened with him," I said, "but if he were to come back, I'd want to be able to explore what our connection could be."

On that Friday morning, the only practice at "non-monogamy" Don and I had under our belt was one sex party we attended. We'd enjoyed being watched while having sex with each other, but we hadn't actually touched anybody else since we'd started dating, and definitely not someone either of us had a genuine connection with.

Don texted again twenty minutes later. Did you ask him out yet?!
No, I replied. I don't know what to suggest.
Just ask him if he wants to get a drink later, Don wrote. Simple.
I glanced at Lukas behind my shoulder and adjusted my beanie.

I raised my stainless steel mug and sipped on my third coffee of the day.

That would be too directly asking him out! I thumbed. What if he's not into me?

There is no way he'd be disappointed if you asked him out, Don replied. Do it now, before you chicken out!

I smiled at my phone and felt another pang. I had no idea how enjoyable it would be to have a partner help me snag a date with a crush. I closed my laptop and slid it in my backpack. If Lukas's answer wasn't positive, I would be seemingly on my way out and would run down the hatch.

When Don and I had matched online, I was twenty-six and had just finished a degree in educational technology. I'd moved to Brooklyn from Montreal for school, and ditched monogamy as soon as I set foot in the city; my newfound anonymity made me feel free to explore parts of myself previously repressed.

Our first date was at an eerily empty wine bar. I sat on a red cushioned bench with my back to the window, and Don sat on a dark leather chair across from me. Large Edison bulbs hung from the wood paneling on the ceilings. I told Don that I was surprised he'd messaged me. "Are you looking for a *committed* non-monogamous relationship?" I said. "Because nothing in your profile says that."

I had been burned many times by people who thought that the *non-monogamous* label on my OkCupid profile meant *casual sex*.

Don reclined in his seat, shifted his knees to the side of the table, and crossed his long legs. He was rocking a seersucker jacket and cowboy boots. Not a lot of men in New York City could pull that off. But he did. Handsomely.

"Honestly," he said, "I've never really thought about non-monogamy before. So I don't know if it's what I'm looking for."

It wasn't the answer I wanted, but I had a weak spot for blue eyes and graying beards.

"Here's what I do know," he continued. "I'm almost thirty-six, and I haven't been truly happy in a relationship for more than a year. There's gotta be something I'm doing wrong."

He told me that his first love cheated on him for years. That he went through two failed engagements before he got married, and filed for divorce less than a year after the wedding. He talked about the life crisis he underwent when he left his Southern Baptist church and became an atheist.

"I've questioned everything I was taught growing up," he said. "Except monogamy. Reading your profile made me curious."

Something about Don's ability to share his experiences with both vulnerability and confidence eased my typical first-date stiffness. I crossed my legs and leaned back, rested my elbow on my hip, holding up my glass of Pinot Noir. I talked openly about my romantic and sexual attraction for women. I was upfront about not wanting kids. I even admitted that I feared growing old alone because I'd felt trapped in the kind of relationship that everyone around me and on TV seemed to find happiness in.

Don and I went on our second date the next evening. On our third date, he invited me to join him on a trip to a research conference in New Orleans. We plunged into unrestrained love.

We got married a year in, not because we were invested in the institution of marriage, but because my visa was expiring, and our love was not.

The night after Lukas showed up on my rooftop, he and I walked around Prospect Park in the chill December air. We sipped cocktails in a two-door garage-turned-speakeasy with copper ceiling tiles and brick walls, where we sat on black stools facing one another, our knees touching. He talked about his job as a technical translator. I loved languages and was impressed he spoke four. He told me about Vienna, I talked about Montreal. I touched his knee, and he leaned a little closer. I tapped the plastic cocktail pick on the side of my empty glass. What was the protocol for bringing up non-monogamy? First date? Was this even a date? Or meaningless flirting between temporary neighbors? Every time I got close to broaching the topic, the words got stuck in my throat.

Later, we stood by the staircase that led to his cousin's floor, unsure of how to fill the charged silence. My studio was on the ground floor. I stepped forward and hugged him.

"Thanks for coming on a neighborhood tour," I said, my voice muffled in my hand-knit scarf.

"Thanks for showing me around," he replied in his delightful accent.

I slowly pulled back, letting my cheek graze his five o'clock shadow. We looked at each other, our faces a few inches apart. Lukas was timid, and obviously had no idea how handsome he was. He raised his hand, very delicately held the side of my glasses frame in between his two fingers, and pushed them back an eighth of an inch on my nose. His lack of assurance was endearing. I leaned forward and put my lips against his. Our kiss was warm, tender, and affectionate. His lips never once tried to open mine wider, which felt like a refreshing change of pace. I felt the full-body swell of elation.

I called Don as soon as I closed my apartment door behind me. He could hear how excited I was. His emotion was difficult to read on the phone. He sounded happy for me, but also uncomfortable.

"How do you feel about me going on a proper date with him tomorrow?" I asked. We'd previously talked about spacing out our dates with others, but Lukas was flying out two days later.

"Hmm..."

I slowly unzipped my coat and I listened to the sound of Don's e-cigarette popping, followed by a long exhale.

"Yeah, it's his last day, you should enjoy him, sweetheart."

The frame of my futon squeaked under me as I climbed onto Lukas, straddling him. He kissed my neck with gentleness and care. His fingertips brushed my back under my shirt, featherlike. He made me feel precious. Adored even.

Don and I had agreed Lukas could come back to my place after dinner, and that heavy make-out was allowed, but nothing under the belt. I knew it was dishonest to keep Lukas in the dark, but I was terrified and I reasoned with myself that it would only be a three-day fling. His flight was the next day, and who knew if he'd even come back to New York.

After Lukas left my apartment, I called a cab and took the forty-five minute trip to Don's place uptown. It was past midnight, but we'd agreed that whoever had a date needed to travel to the other at the end of the night. I dozed in and out on the Westside Highway, my forehead on the cool window, piers and boats flashing when I opened my eyes, lights from buildings on the New Jersey shoreline reflecting on the Hudson River.

Weeks after Lukas returned to Vienna, we were still texting daily. He sent me messages like I can't stop thinking about you, but the guilt churning my stomach stopped me from writing I can't stop thinking about you either.

I sunk into a beanbag chair in my office, computer on my lap. The hood of my sweatshirt covered my greasy hair and signaled to my colleagues that I was hungover and they should avoid talking to me. Someone had brought their leftover Valentine's Day treats in a bowl. I put a fistful in my hoodie pocket, then peeled a pink Hershey Chocolate Kiss and let it melt slowly on my tongue. When Lukas sent me a message saying he would come back to New York soon, I was tired enough—and perhaps had sufficient residual alcohol in my system—that the potential consequences of telling the truth were diminished in my brain. I decided to rip off the bandage.

I'm not interested in traditional dating, I typed with no assurance. My colleague's chihuahua ran across the kitchen space, his little nails clacking on the floor. And it's something people don't expect of me. So when I meet someone new, it's difficult to give them the real picture of what my life looks like and what I want. Does that make sense?

I think so, he answered, clearly not thinking so.

I continued: And you seem traditional in your approach to dating, I guess.

Traditional is the only way I know, he wrote.

His response charmed me. He could have gotten defensive, reading my statement as a reproach. Instead, he showed openness and curiosity. I feared he'd close up once he heard more, but I pressed on.

Well, I wrote. I'm interested in non-monogamy.

I held my breath. A colleague wearing large over-the-ears headphones sat in the beanbag next to mine. We nodded at each other. I stared at the moving dots on my screen.

You should have just said that from the start, he wrote. Now I feel like an idiot.

No! Why would you feel like an idiot?

Because I got too attached too quickly and treated you like a delicate flower, and it's not what you wanted.

I understood he felt stupid because he equated my want for non-monogamy with a want for no-strings-attached sex.

No, I love the way you treated me, I typed. I'm not interested in casual sex. I just don't believe I can limit myself to loving one person at a time for the rest of my life.

I kept typing, wanting to finally get it all out. Two people in coats walked past, heading towards the elevator. And, I wrote, I'm seeing someone. It's only been five months, but it feels serious. We've known we wanted to try non-monogamy since the beginning though, and he knows I've been on dates with you. I didn't know how to tell you all that, especially since you were only in the city for a few days. I'm really sorry.

I sank deeper into the red beanbag, heavy with shame. I'd wanted to explore polyamory as a means of reaching total honesty in all my relationships, yet in my first attempt, I'd deceived someone that I really, really liked. Everyone else I'd met in the two years prior had known exactly what to expect—it was clearly explained in my dating profile. But in all of those interactions, I was inviting someone to go on the journey *with* me—without any existing partners in tow. This was the first time I'd met someone organically and invited them to become a second partner.

Yeah, interesting, he wrote back. I actually believe that too.

Hope rose up my spine, straightening it a bit as he continued.

> It's a fact that monogamy in humans isn't
> natural, that's not how we evolved. So I
> understand. I'm pretty sure I told you the first
> time we went out that I don't intend to get
> married. That's why.

On the other side of the office, someone was playing ping pong.

Because you don't believe in monogamy? I asked. Not wanting to get married and being non-monogamous are two very separate things, so it's not what I had understood you meant.

Lukas explained that the biggest point of tension with his ex was that she complained he wanted too much time alone. Lukas was an introvert, and spent large chunks of his free days on his computer. What would it have been like had she had another partner to keep her busy half the time? Though he wasn't sure if non-monogamy was really what he wanted, given the transatlantic nature of our relationship, he was willing to try.

Lukas stood in the hallway in a black coat holding a dripping umbrella. I invited him into Don's apartment and closed the door behind him. We stood by the entryway in front of the shotgun kitchen. The living room and bedroom were around an elbow corner. I put my arms around Lukas's neck and went in to kiss him. He jerked back as soon as my lips touched his.

"What are you doing?" he whispered in a panic, shooting glances toward the living room.

I felt his shoulders and arms tense through his coat. "It's okay," I said, reassuring him. "We don't have to do anything different than when it's just the two of us."

Don turned the corner in jeans, a black t-shirt and his beloved cowboy boots. "Welcome, welcome!" he said with a wide smile. He outstretched his hand, Lukas shook it, and Don patted him on the back in a half hug. It was the end of Lukas's first week back in New York, and our bond had rapidly developed. He was scheduled to leave in a few days.

An hour later, I could tell Lukas had relaxed. "Thank you for accepting the invitation and being so lovely," Don told Lukas, while dipping a tuna maki piece in soy sauce. "It's important for me to have the opportunity to get to know Alex's boyfriend."

A shock of surprise and joy spread through my body. I set my chopsticks on my plate. Don and I had never discussed labels for our other partners, and hearing *boyfriend* from his mouth made it feel more serious, more committed. By putting the word *boyfriend* on the table, Don had given us his blessing.

"I was a little nervous," Lukas said, "but this is nice."

At the end of the evening, Lukas and Don made plans to play tennis the next day. I was elated that their first meeting went so well. I was doing it! Polyamory the way it was supposed to be done. Everyone knew what was going on, and no one was lying.

Lukas pulled on his brown ankle boots by the door and Don hugged him. This time, it was a real hug.

A few months later, Don and I sat at the table in the corner of his living room, each scrolling through the calendars on our phones, preparing for one of Lukas's visits. I pushed my half-eaten lasagna plate to the side.

"We have Broadway tickets Thursday," I said, "but I was wondering if I could bring him to the movies Friday. He wants to see *Fantastic Beasts*."

"I'd rather you don't spend two nights in a row with him," Don said. "Can you see the movie Saturday?"

"No, he's busy Saturday," I replied. I sucked my upper lip and exhaled through my nose. The ecstasy I'd been feeling for weeks had slowly become mixed with low-level dread. In addition to this *no consecutive dates* rule, we also couldn't do sleepovers. I accepted these rules, but wished I could have more freedom. Things felt more complicated since Lukas stayed in my building when he was in town. Don felt a certain lack of control.

Of course, I was in the thralls of "new relationship energy," and I would have devoted every free moment or thought to Lukas during the short times we shared a continent. But I knew that whatever constraints I accepted in this relationship would be available for me to deploy when Don inevitably found someone he wanted to spend large swaths of his time with.

"I won't do the movie then," I said, and removed the event from my calendar.

Don put his hand on my knee under the table and leaned in to kiss my neck.

"Je t'aime," he said in my ear. I loved hearing him say it in French, always with an elongated *je*.

"I love you too," I said, and ran my nose against his before kissing his lips.

"Every time you meet someone new," I complained to Don while he slid out of his jeans on the other side of the bed, "I have to go through the anxious period of wondering what this person will want, what your relationship will look like, worrying about how it will affect our life. Whether you'll start spending half your weekends with her." I leaned against two pillows, took my glasses off and stretched my arm up to put them on top of the tall dresser that I used as a night stand. "It's much more exhausting than you dealing with Lukas's visits every couple of months!"

Don tossed his jeans, t-shirt and socks on the armchair in the corner, pulled the comforter back, and sat in bed in his boxers.

"You're *in love* with Lukas," he replied, gesticulating with the air conditioning remote in hand, before turning the air on. "Every time he visits, it's like another honeymoon for you two. I haven't even come close to that with anyone I've seen. You look at him the way you looked at me when we first met. *That's* harder."

Even though I knew that my feelings for Lukas and investment in our relationship didn't make me any less committed to Don, I struggled at trusting that it would be the same for Don. We enacted rules that reinforced the notion that ours was the *primary* relationship. We didn't even question our approach, because it felt safer, and it allowed us to function in the world the way "normal" couples did.

Lukas was my age and height, he was thin, and had a certain innocence and wonder to him that I loved. During his visits, I worked from home more often and we went on coffee walks in the afternoons, and found alleyways to make out. I'd press him against the wall and feel how nervous he was. His favorite movie was Beauty and the Beast, which I bought so we could watch it together on one of his visits. He was asleep before Belle was imprisoned; I closed the laptop, pulled the covers to his shoulders, and spooned him. He let his beard and chest hair grow because that's what I preferred. He started working out daily and said he was trying to sculpt his body for me—while it's not something I had asked him to do and I liked his body how it was, seeing his devotion and hard work made me feel adored, powerful. With him, I felt in control, worshipped, served.

Once, I entered the bathroom as he was getting out of the shower. I pulled his towel and let it fall to the floor, and despite his worry that we didn't have time, I rolled a condom down his cock, pressed my hands against the wall and told him to push into me. Afterwards, he said he loved how I didn't give him a choice.

Don was almost a decade older than me, six inches taller, and the first partner I'd ever trusted like a mentor. He was confident and self-assured, but only rarely cocky. He spoke about his emotions easily and often understood mine before I expressed them. He was established in his career, and felt responsibility for the well-being of the other people in his life, caring for them in an almost paternal way: with his mentees at his research center, his mother, and me. In my previous relationships, I always felt I was the one who had to help my partner get their life together. I'd never realized how replenishing it could be for me to be held and led, until I met Don.

Despite the exhaustion that came from managing everyone's emotions and needs, the love I felt for and from my two partners was indescribable; my body could barely hold it. I felt more whole, because different parts of myself came out of the distinct kind of intimacy I had with each. Even though I had to navigate rules rooted in fear, I had never felt more free.

"I have something to tell you," Don said, as I laid my head on my pillow to read before bed. He sat at the foot of the bed, and squeezed my ankle through the white comforter. We had just come back from seeing a play, a surprise outing Don organized as my slightly early Christmas gift. "I hope I'm doing the right thing by telling you," he said. "But I've been sitting on this all week, and I worry that you'll be mad at me for not having told you when you find out."

I sat up, not sure how alarmed I should be. Don knew that radical transparency was something I required in order to maintain trust. In the past, I'd been upset when he omitted small details when recalling his dates or conveying other potentially upsetting information, categorizing them as lies.

"It's Lukas," he said. "He wants to break up with you."

My heart dropped. "What? He told you that?" I asked.

"Yeah. He called me on Monday."

"*Three* days ago?"

"I know, I know," Don said. "He told me he'd call you that night, then the day after, and now it seems like you two haven't talked all week." He took a long drag on his e-cigarette, and exhaled slowly, twisting his mouth to direct the smoke to the side without breaking eye contact with me. "I really hope I'm doing the right thing by telling you."

I'd been dating Lukas for a year, and while he and Don got along, they'd never talked on the phone and rarely texted in between his visits.

"Why would he call *you*?" I asked.

"He said he wanted to make sure I'd be available to be with you when he would tell you. He was crying."

"But what did he *say*?" I asked, in tears. "I thought things were going well." I pulled a paper tissue out of the box on my nightstand. Don looked powerless. He shouldn't have been the one having to explain why Lukas was breaking up with me.

"Do you want to see what he texted before he asked to call me?"

I nodded.

Hey Don, Lukas wrote. I need some advice. I need to end things with Alex. The last time I was in NYC I went on a few dates with someone else, and it reminded me about the things I'm missing. This isn't a decision I wanted to make because she's absolutely amazing, and I don't know how to do it.

He then apologized to Don, explaining that he understood that it would impact him too, that he knew I'd take it hard. The resentment I'd initially felt melted into heartbroken endearment. I found it sweet that Lukas trusted Don enough to talk to him openly.

That sweetness only made it harder and more confusing. I felt like Lukas and I had just hit our stride, and being the hinge partner in our V-shaped relationship was no longer draining; Don had even reached out to him two months prior to coordinate a surprise visit for me—I'd been missing Lukas terribly, and he'd wanted to cheer me up.

I had mailed Lukas's Christmas present earlier that day: a handmade beanie with a small leather tag with A + L stamped on it. I wished I'd known this was coming. I would have kept the beanie so I could wear it around the house and mope.

Lukas had been nothing but patient and understanding, and his text to Don confirmed my suspicion that our rules had been deeply unfair to him. He had willingly accepted them, but we hadn't given him the room to push back. Still, I couldn't believe he'd break up with me for someone he barely knew. When this colleague of his had invited him to go to Coney Island, Lukas had immediately messaged me and asked if I thought she was asking him out, and if it would be okay for him to go. I was thrilled that he was finally interested in dating someone other than me, and hoped it would make things feel more balanced between us.

"But they haven't even kissed yet!" I told Don between sobs. "They went on *two* dates! He didn't even try to really explain it to her!"

Don crawled next to me and wrapped his arms around me. He lay there all night, completely silent, squeezing me tightly as I wept. I couldn't believe that I was being dumped by Lukas, while he slept, four thousand miles away.

# the bobby pin

I slipped two gold bobby pins in my hair and picked up a third. I froze. The next one in my hand was black. I realized it must be Aly's—Don's new girlfriend. They'd been dating for a month. She had beautiful dark hair, long and thick. The kind I spent my teenage years envying. I looked around the bathroom, wondering where to store the bobby pin. Through the open window, I heard laughs from Columbia students out for boozy brunch.

Finding reminders of Don's other partners gave me momentary pangs of jealousy. When I noticed the bedsheets had been changed, I imagined Don having loud, vigorous sex. Or when wine glasses were placed on the wrong shelf, I pictured a girlfriend pouring cabernet wearing one of Don's button-downs like a dress over her naked body. I had learned to acknowledge these intrusive images, and breathe through them slowly and deeply.

I'd been with Don for three years. He met Aly after both he and I had gone through difficult breakups with our respective partners, and we were grappling with how to make real room for others in our lives. Fortunately, Aly lived with her fiancé, so she was less threatening to me than the unpartnered women Don had briefly dated.

I held the bobby pin between my thumb and index finger, scanning the bathroom. I opened the vanity, but it would have been odd to place it between cleaning products and a toilet plunger. I opened the medicine cabinet, but if I placed it between Don's hair paste and nail clippers, would I be officially giving Aly a space in our home? If I threw the bobby pin away, was I failing at polyamory? Until I could decide what to do, I placed it back in the stack of pins I kept on the windowsill.

Three weeks earlier, after Don's first date with Aly, I sat on the toilet and opened the calendar app on my phone. I noticed a new event that Friday in blue, the color of Don's calendar. It was titled *Aly?*

I washed my hands quickly and dried them on my jeans while I walked across the hall to the living room. "Did you schedule a date this weekend?" I asked Don, standing in the doorway. He picked up the TV controller from the metal library card cabinet that served as a coffee table and pressed pause on a documentary about Ancient Rome.

"Oh right! Well, not yet," he said, "but Aly was only free Friday night this week. It's tough to say no when it's only our second date... Maybe I can see her right after work and get back here early so we can spend a chunk of the evening together?"

I had always fiercely guarded weekends. Don is an introvert—his energy level is correlated with the number of words he has spoken on any given day. After being promoted at his research center, his meeting-packed weekdays left him drained. His

Sundays were reserved for watching football or documentaries to recharge for the week. Friday evenings and Saturdays were our peak quality time, and I insisted he ask my permission before scheduling a date on those days.

"I guess that's fine," I said begrudgingly, crossing my arms and leaning my shoulder on the doorway. "But it would be the second Friday in a row you see her. Can you make it clear that our dates with others are usually on weeknights?"

Don acquiesced, but my jaw remained clenched.

I hadn't met Aly yet. The *meet-the-spouse* step of the relationship was a delicate one, and we usually waited at least five or six dates. To me, she was the shadow of a selfish, needy villain, threatening to take something irreplaceable away from me. Don pushed play. Caesar was marching legions of soldiers across a river.

After Don's fourth date with Aly, he carefully initiated a poly rules check-in over breakfast: "Aly explained that she isn't comfortable having sex with a partner without sleepovers." He paused. I walked to the window behind me and pulled back the blackout curtain. The morning sun was blinding, even in the winter. Don squinted. "I know more sleepovers is also something Lukas wanted with you," he said. "So I wanted to see what you think."

I sat down on my mustard chair. My ears pulsed. I looked down at my scrambled eggs and said nothing.

I was dismayed to be spending our Saturday morning talking about his girlfriend. I'd asked him just last week to stop playing her album over the Bluetooth speaker because, while yes, it was good and exactly my kind of folk music, I didn't need to hear her sing when we were having a tête-à-tête.

Don took a bite. In our silence, I heard Lukas's most devastating reason for breaking up with me: "It took a whole year before I was allowed to spend the night and wake up with you." Don chewed slowly, his eyes surveying mine.

"I'll think about it," I said, then stood up and walked my plate to the garbage can. I pressed my foot on the pedal and dumped the rest of my eggs.

Don and I had allowed a handful of sleepovers with our other partners, but they were reserved for special occasions. We typically coordinated so we would both have them on the same night. Initially, this was one of the rules that was most important to me; sharing sleep felt more intimate than sex. Don was territorial about the bathroom: I was the first partner he showered with regularly, so this felt special to him, and he preferred I didn't share cleaning intimacy with anyone else.

We traded sleepover and shower privileges, treating our partners like subordinates who didn't deserve a seat at the negotiation table.

Don's girlfriend before Aly, Bridget, lived alone, so their dates and occasional sleepovers always happened at her place. I had a beautiful relationship with Bridget, but I'd never found her threatening—she and her primary partner maintained a strict hierarchy. How would I feel with Aly sleeping in *our* bed? Doing her hair in *our* bathroom?

Even though Don and I kept both of our apartments and spent half the week apart, we shared our homes; we rented the studio on Airbnb on weekends, we split the combined rent in half, chose furniture together, and referred to our apartments by the name of the street they were on, not "Alex's place" and "Don's place." It felt remarkably sustainable to share life-long goals with Don while maintaining independence and the excitement of missing him weekly.

Aly and I made plans to meet for coffee a few days later; our first time meeting each other. I arrived early and sat by a floor-to-ceiling window on the second floor, overlooking a prewar building covered by green scaffolding. I recognized Aly from her pictures as she ascended the staircase. I waved and she walked gracefully but purposefully towards me, her steps clacking on the wood floor. We were the only customers upstairs and there was no music playing. She wore black knee-high boots over black pants and a long beige coat.

"So nice to finally meet you!" she said in a high-pitched voice, with so much enthusiasm I wondered if it was authentic.

Her long frizz-free hair and her red lipstick were impeccable. I admired how put together she was and momentarily felt self-conscious about my messy ponytail and my plain tee-shirt.

Aly listened intently to my *how I ended up trying non-monogamy* summary (the inevitable introductory topic). She nodded her head energetically and raised her eyebrows in quick intervals. She crushed every two-second silence with a follow up question. Lost in my own anxiety, it hadn't occurred to me that *she* may be nervous to meet *me*.

I listened to her telling me the highlights of her life story. Our conversation was punctuated by the occasional hammering from the construction site across the street. Like Don, Aly had grown up in the South, and had experiences imprinted in her that I could never fully understand—similar to how Don would never feel my French-Canadian culture in his bones. She had gone back to school to study creative writing, and I was excited to have someone to talk to about my side writing projects. I walked to the bathroom, passed a large decorative wall quilt with tones of red and ochre. While washing my hands, I began to focus on what Aly could add to my life instead of what she might take away. It had been surprisingly hard for me to make platonic friendships in the city. Unless there was potential for romantic love or sex, no new connection had room for me on their calendar. Even though Aly and I were strangers, her budding romance with Don gave us a reason to prioritize developing a unique kind of friendship. After just a half-hour, I felt my abdomen relax. Aly was now a *person* to me. A person with a nervous propensity to fill silences, a self-consciousness about not finishing college until her thirties, and hopes for a new creative future outside of music. And—just like me—she was on a path to figuring out what kind of relationship would make her happy.

Two days after I found Aly's bobby pin, I was folding laundry and noticed an unfamiliar neon orange sports bra. Then a new tank top, shorts, and socks. I scanned my body, expecting the usual pangs of jealousy. None. I walked to the living room with the pile of workout clothing in hand. Don was on the recliner reading something on his phone, probably a depressing article about climate change. I walked closer to him, and stood at his side, holding out the items. "These are Aly's, right?" I asked.

"Oh...that's right," he answered slowly, his voice lower. He pushed the recliner closed with his legs and tapped his pocket in search of his e-cigarette. He stood up, slid his fingers between the seat and the armrest, and found it. He took a long drag, looking into my eyes, still standing. "We played tennis," he said apologetically.

He clearly hadn't considered the emotional implications of tossing Aly's clothes in our hamper.

"I'll put them in your workout clothes drawer for next time she needs it. Does that work?"

"That sounds great, sweetheart." There was surprise and gratitude in his voice. He sat back down.

Don *loved* tennis, and I refused to touch a racket. Any activity that required me to hit a moving target with an object or a limb gave me a panic attack. I felt relieved that Don had finally found a tennis partner.

I, too, had wished for more freedom with my ex. I knew what it was like to love under the weight of rules; forcing our other partners into tight little boxes that left no room for deep intimacy and commitment. It left no room for *their* needs. No wonder Lukas felt secondary. Had we met when I was farther along in my polyamorous journey, might we still be together?

Don and I had built security in our relationship, and it was time to loosen the hierarchy we had been operating under. Even though I knew that traditional expectations of love were still ingrained somewhere in me, I aspired to a more egalitarian polyamory.

I folded Aly's exercise clothes, and as I placed them neatly into the drawer, I felt a new kind of lightness. I actually *wanted* her relationship with Don to have the room it needed to grow. I returned to the living room and told Don they should have sleepovers whenever they wanted.

The next time I reached for a bobby pin and picked up the black one, it had been more than a week since its existence had frozen me.

I popped it in my hair with a smile.

# fragments for my metamour (do i still call you my metamour?)

You show up to my thirty-first birthday, on the farm I work at for the season in the Hudson Valley. *This is Aly, my partner's partner*, I tell everyone. You're wearing black jean shorts and your great-grandfather's cowboy boots. I hug you and your hair smells of coconut. The farm crew is buzzing around: one is grilling burgers, one is peeling garlic to make aioli, another is making a salad with lettuce and cherry tomatoes harvested that day. It's a little much that you put on red lipstick for a farm party, but you always wear makeup. You're stylish and shiny in contrast with our gritty barn kitchen and my dirty jeans.

Ten of us sit on logs around the fire after dusk and share art: Someone performs a traditional Egyptian dance, someone shares a folk tale, some play music, some share jokes. I read new fragments that I'll later turn into essays.

When your turn comes, you pull your guitar onto your lap and address the group. "Something I admire about Alex," you say, "is their ability to be honest and open about their emotions. They're not scared to show vulnerable parts of themself, which is endearing, and not something I do easily." You shuffle on your log, turn to me. "So this song is about vulnerability." You hold my gaze, and smile shyly. You are still a close acquaintance, not yet an intimate friend. There is a certain wall around you that I can't crack. But for the first time, I see tenderness in your eyes. I know that you have a practiced stage banter from those years touring with your former band, but your face is softer in the firelight than I've ever seen it, and it seems like this is the way you express uncomfortable feelings best. By inviting you to come Upstate and stay with Don and me in my tiny farmhouse suite, and to take part in my birthday celebration, I hoped I'd send you the message that I wanted to move towards something more familial. Your words make me believe you are ready for it.

When Don tells me he'll see you on Thursday this week, I stay silent for a moment, trying to resist the urge to question his choice. We are in bed, he's about to read *The Hidden Life of Trees* aloud for me until I drift off. Even though I no longer guard weekend days for myself, Don continues to schedule his dates with you on weeknights. I've been with him for four years; you've been dating him for almost a year.

"Maybe Aly would prefer Friday," I venture. "She doesn't get to see you much on weekends. And I know she's usually alone on Fridays because Jake is with Krista."

Don later tells me I was right, that you were happy he offered Friday. It's the first time I've ever predicted one of your needs; it makes me feel closer to you, like I'm a better metamour. I can't pinpoint when it happened, but my protectiveness over my own needs has transferred to yours. I now operate from a place of abundance, as opposed to scarcity or fear, knowing that there's plenty of love to go around. But I also worry about Don being a good partner to you, and it reflecting well on *me*. Why do I feel that your contentment with him is partly my responsibility?

When you and Jake decide to "move out together" and rent separate places in the same building, I come to your new apartment with rolling trays and tarps full of paint stains. Neither of us trust Don to hang a frame, let alone maneuver a roller full of indigo paint in your small studio. *I'm always a mess when I move*, you say, looking at the piles of boxes in the corners, sighing and massaging your neck with one hand. Your eyes are puffy, and it's the first time I see you without mascara. *Do you want me to lead this and tell you what to do?* I ask. Your shoulders soften. *That would be great*, you say. We crouch in the corner and I teach you how to cut in with a paintbrush, starting with the baseboards. I roll the paint roller back and forth on the grooved part of the tray, and begin applying paint to the wall. We hear voices every time people walk by your ground floor windows. We cracked them open to help with the paint smell, even though it's January. I try spreading the paint evenly on the wall but the roller leaves darker strikes everywhere. I'm nervous it won't come out even; it's too early in our relationship for me to be responsible for any imperfections in the first apartment that has ever been wholly yours.

But once it's dry, it looks perfect.

In the winter, we start meeting weekly to support one another with our writing. The night before our first session, you send me your address. "It's Aly," Don says, and hands me my phone that was plugged in next to him on the couch. I put my book down on the cushion next to me.

Thanks! I text back I'd already labeled your address as "Aly" in my Google Maps app.

Hahaha, you reply. This is one of the many reasons you and Don work.

How many times did he ask for your new address? I ask.

Every. Time.

I laugh. You moved almost four months ago.

Yep, that sounds right, I text.

That man has a special kind of obliviousness, you write.

I laugh out loud again.

"What are you giggling at?" Don asks. I look up and smile. He is playing Chess on his phone, still wearing his headband down to his eyebrows even though he finished his workout hours ago.

"Oh, nothing." I answer. "Aly and I are talking about how charming you are, that's all."

We sit on the floor against your emerald velvet loveseat, eating Indian food out of takeout containers. You've done some impressive work in your studio: your four guitars adorn the walls, your books are organized by jacket color, and you added chic-looking peel and stick backsplash in your galley kitchen. Even your cat tower looks fancy. You're a Facebook Marketplace pro, you often say.

*You know*, I say after I'm done reading your latest draft, *it's funny that I'm unable to write about my kinks but I write at length about my polyamory, but for you it's the opposite.*

We try to self-diagnose. The answer is shame. It always is.

While we write at my kitchen island, you get off your stool to get your homemade Kombucha out of the fridge, then circle around the island and pour some in my mason jar, your free hand briefly touching my back, before sitting and pouring into yours. Mango is my favorite. I haven't had alcohol in almost four years. You've been sober for eight. I sometimes wonder if we would have had sex by now if we still drank.

We take a hiking and writing trip Upstate, without Don. We decide to stay an extra night because of a nasty spring rainstorm passing through. On the brown leather couch in our Airbnb, we face one another, each reclined on an armrest. You're wearing a red plaid shirt over a black sleeveless top, and your hair is tucked in a disheveled bun.

For the first time, I am struck by your beauty. I try to write but I keep looking up to look at your focused face. I rarely see you without makeup, and you've never worn your glasses with me. I think everyone is alluring with glasses on. Writing together like this, in our bedtime clothes, feels sensual. The rainfall accompanies our piano-for-writing playlist, and I sip on my lemon tea and you sip on your mint tea.

You tell Jake you want to transition out of a romantic and sexual relationship with him but continue living in the same building and co-parenting the pets. He agrees, but starts acting out and you're miserable. You send me an audio note describing how he refuses to talk to you and even pretends you're not there when you go up to the fifth floor to pick up your dog at his apartment, and how he took off his engagement ring and left it prominently on the kitchen counter by the door. I listen to your note in the hot July sun on the back balcony at my Airbnb while I'm visiting family in Montreal. Downstairs neighbors are digging in their yard and laying landscaping tile, and next-door neighbors are playing loud rock and sitting in an inflatable pool drinking canned beer.

"I think I'm probably gonna see how it goes for the next few weeks," you say in your note, and let out a short sigh. "Like as the immediate discomfort passes, to see if this settles into something that feels completely manageable, and if it's not, then I'll fucking break my lease. My building has just totally revamped the whole thing because they wanna jack the rent up when people's leases end so I think my landlord would probably be delighted."

I type a text response.

> **ME**
> Ok I just finished your audio. Yeah honestly, you could totally tell your landlord look, I'll leave and you'll rent it higher. To negotiate.

**YOU**
Yep

> **ME**
> And also, starting grad school will be really intense for you.

**YOU**
Oh fuuuuuhk I forgot that starts in a month

> **ME**
> So... I don't know how much bandwidth you'll have to put up with Jake's insecurities.

**YOU**
Fair point
Hmm.

**ME**

I mean it may be too quick to make a
decision before you start
But I've seen you move
And I've felt how anxious you were
And grad school + emotions with Jake +
working + moving + managing passing
animals back and forth or splitting them
between you

**YOU**

Yeah! For being someone who's moved
around as much as I have I kind of freak out a
surprising amount.

A half hour later, I send you an apartment listing in our neighborhood in New York City. A large ground floor studio with a
decorative fireplace, *two* closets and a separate kitchen with a
black and white tiled floor. You add two exclamation points to the
link.

**YOU**

I just looked on streeteasy and didn't see this
one!

I'm shocked that you're seriously considering moving closer
to us.

**ME**

I love that you were looking

## fragments for my metamour

I heart your message, slide my glasses up on my head, and reapply sunscreen on my sweaty face. I broke up with Cara six months ago, and now that I'm recovered, I have an influx of time and energy that I naturally redirect toward you.

You become my and Don's main conversation topic.

At bedtime, after I turn on the window air conditioning unit and Don takes my weighted blanket out of the closet to lay it on me in bed, I ask him if he's heard from you this evening. He sits on the edge of the bed next to me and shakes his head.

"She told Jake that she wants to move uptown and split the pets," I say.

"Oh wow," he says. "I knew she was thinking about it but I didn't think she'd do it so quickly."

It surprises me that you told me before telling Don. It makes me feel special, like I'm as important as him even though you two have been romantic for two years now. Though I sometimes worry that our deepening bond is just a way for you to rebound, to fill the space that Jake left until you're back on your feet. I think maybe I should be careful, not dive into an interdependent friendship too fast, but I don't know how.

Don kisses my forehead, my cheeks, my lips, and I kiss his cheeks. "Sleep well," he says, then turns off the lamp and closes the sliding bedroom door behind him.

I pick you up after a medical appointment on the Upper East Side, because they gave you a sedative for a minor procedure. I'm impressed by the waiting room, which has wood paneling, a stone gray tiled floor, and warm lighting.

"You're *picking up* Alexandra, or *you're* Alexandra?" the receptionist asks, squinting at my ID.

"Both. I say. Picking up Alexandra *Tadros*."

"Oh," she says without conviction. I make a mental note to tell you about this when you're no longer high, because we sporadically remember that we both have the same legal first name and it always makes us chuckle.

We walk out of the building and wait for a cab in the shade of a tree. The street is quiet.

"Whatever drugs they gave me are stronger than I thought," you say, avoiding my gaze. "I don't think I can talk much."

I know that you're self-conscious about the effects of the sedative and whether you'll look high in front of me. It's the first time you take any altering substance in nine years.

"Don't talk, then."

In the cab, you put your hand on mine, resting on the seat between us.

"Thank you Alex," you softly say.

You always say my name after a *thank you* when your gratitude goes deep.

"Of course," I reply. "I'm here for you." You squeeze my fingers, then put your hand back on your lap, and turn to the window as we pass by the geometric gates of the Robert F. Kennedy Bridge.

"Are you a couple?" the comedian on stage asks, pointing at you and me. We are sitting in the first row at a queer comedy show at Dixon Place on the Lower East Side. The lounge is narrow, with a bar at one end and a straight piano at the other, and feels like a living room. The performer wears striped overalls and stands in front of green velvet curtains and on a red patterned rug, speaking into a mic. The ten people in the audience sit on mismatched wooden chairs. Six of them are performers in the line up, and I feel uncomfortable under observation in such a small crowd. I stop breathing, smile crisply, and turn to you. We look at each other for long seconds, unsure what to say.

"Okay, no then" the comedian declares, and pivots towards the only other pair in the audience. "What about you two, are you a couple?"

I exhale. The answer isn't yes, but it feels incorrect to say *no*.

I rent a log cabin month-to-month in the Catskills to property hunt, and because I can't handle the city anymore. Don and I have been looking at land with a couple of close friends for a while. We want to live with family, friends, partners. Now that you can work remotely, you officially join in and spend more and more time Upstate with me. Sometimes with Don, sometimes without. You never feel like company.

We often write on the couch in front of the imposing buck head with eight point antlers and the miniature bear standing next to the wood stove and feel observed. One morning, I discover a tick embedded right below my right butt-cheek and you haven't had coffee yet but you spring into action and tell me to lay on all fours on the couch in my underwear. *We have reached a new level of intimacy*, I say while you gently tug on the live tick with tweezers, and we laugh. One cold fall night, I build a fire for you in the yard and you burn mementos from your relationship with Jake. You sob and I put my arm around you, watching the flames melt your past. When the first snow comes, we make snow angels and Casino jumps and rolls around us, sneaking in warm licks on our cheeks.

I pull into the Price Chopper parking lot Upstate. You're in the passenger seat, and Casino is in the back seat chewing on a squeaky rainbow llama.

"I hate large grocery stores," I say, looking at the massive building with a blue tin roof. "But I guess in the country it'll be our only option."

"I like going to chain grocery stores," you say. "It's soothing."

I am aghast. I shift the car in park, unbuckle, and turn to you. "Soothing?" I ask. "How can it be *soothing*?"

"I think it's because when I was touring I found it comforting that all grocery stores were the same." You unbuckle your seatbelt and pull on the Catskills Unity beanie I gifted you for Christmas. "I would often take my time and go through every aisle, listening to music on my headphones or talking to a friend from home."

"Just *thinking* of a grocery store makes me anxious," I say. "Too many people, too many sounds, too many choices. And the fluorescent lighting is depressing. It tires me in a weird way."

"Do you want to wait in the car while I go in?" you ask.

"Oh, I didn't mean to make it sound like I was asking you to go," I say.

"No I know, but I'm happy to. Grocery Shopping can be *my* thing!" you exclaim before opening the door. "Text me if you think of anything else you want."

My heart melts and I thank you. I stretch to pet Casino's head in the back, then reach into my backpack on the floor and pull a book out, *The 2000s Made Me Gay*. I rest it open against the wheel. I glance up as you disappear through the automatic doors, and recline my backrest a touch.

I step on the platform at the top of Bald Mountain, cold air pumping into my lungs in short breaths. I pull my neck gaiter up to my nose; as soon as I stepped out of the woods, the wind aggressively picked up. Standing under the abandoned chairlift, the rusty metal frame of each wooden chair gently swinging in the wind, I take my phone out of my coat pocket to snap a picture of the gray mountains with leafless trees and powdered spots. I see your name on my locked screen and forget about the picture. You sent me two text messages while I hiked up: a picture of the stack of books you brought to the cabin for the week, sitting next to my own pile on the coffee table. I'll tell you what, you wrote. Our future farm will have the BEST library.

I smile wide and the cold hurts my teeth. Mixing books feels very intimate to me.

I pull my thin glove to free my right thumb, then I do the same for my left. I type slowly, my thumbs stiff. I have absolutely fantasized about our joint library in the barn.

Alone in my bed, at six in the morning, I feel a familiar intrusive thought emerging, but this time I don't push it away. I stretch my arm to turn off my white noise machine sitting on the log headboard. I roll on my side and hug one of my pillows, closing my eyes again. I have to admit to myself that my feelings for you have been evolving, and what I thought was purely platonic love may be morphing into desire for a more physical love. I think about our coffee shop outing from yesterday, and how nice it would have been to hold your hand when we walked to the counter, past the mismatched tables and antique coffee pots, and ordered your vanilla oat latte and my decaf Americano. And after you gave the wired barista your rainbow mug that I gifted you, and he complimented it and took it to the espresso machine on the side, I could have pulled you towards me and raised my chin slightly to kiss your lips, and maybe your fingers could have brushed the shaved hair above my neck, and when the barista handed us our drinks he could have said *So. Cute. So Cute!* in his typical animated cadence.

I flip on my back and pull the wolf quilt to my chin. The pale blue light of dawn peaks through the green mountains painted on the closed window shutters. I press the side button on my phone: It's now past seven. I don't *want* to be attracted to you. I've been preaching that metamour relationships are the best thing in polyamory. I've been telling people that not all polyamorists end up dating each other. But here I am, longing for a girlfriend and missing sex with women. And I know you miss queer sex, too. Are we living a romantic comedy cliché, when two close friends take the whole movie to realize they have been looking for each other? Our relationship has evolved into something so difficult to grasp, describe, understand.

I sit on the couch between you and Casino, your dog that is now mine part-time. The bear and the buck mounted on the wall watch us watch an episode of *Insecure* on my laptop, propped on the coffee table. You're wearing your glasses and your cropped gray hoodie with loose sweatpants. You react dramatically to every plot twist, pressing your fingers into my thigh, turning to me, your mouth agape, your brown freckles stretched. You repeatedly erupt in loud laughter. You usually speak gently, slowly; you only get this way when you're immersed in a show or movie. I laugh with you.

You enter my bedroom at three in the morning, your hair in a messy ponytail, your eyes half closed. Canned laughs and comedic voices play on my phone at low volume.

"Don is snoring so loudly," you say grumpily, sliding under the covers.

I pause the sitcom and put the phone on my nightstand between the white noise machine and my sleeping pills bottle.

You press your back against me. I fold my left arm under my pillow, and my right arm pulls you in tightly. You drift to sleep in less than a minute. We breathe in unison; your back and my chest expand and press into each other at regular intervals. My left arm is falling asleep, my cheek is itchy, but I stay put. I usually never fall asleep without a show, but I do this time.

Your legs are crossed under your classical guitar, and your russet boot moves slowly in the air to the rhythm of your melodic finger-picking. It's an old song of yours, but you chose it for me, for my thirty-first birthday. A wistful and haunting arpeggio draws everyone in, closer to the warmth of the fire. Everyone is completely still on their log.

> *and when the storm rolls through*
> *I wanna take care of you*
> *Shelter you*

I no longer hear the fire crackling or the crickets chirp. Your voice is soulful, your gravelly lows are rich, alluring. You pluck your strings and gently rock back and forth. I notice a slight ache in my cheeks; I've been smiling at you during the whole song.

> *won't you come inside*
> *Rest your head here*
> *Lay on by the fire*
> *Cause you could come inside*
> *There's nothing to fear*
> *Just lay on by,*
> *lay on by the fire*
>
> *We've got nothing to fear love*

# wide plank floors

A quarter of my father died on October 14, 2010. I had just turned twenty-one.

When I entered his hospital room, my mother was standing in the back corner firmly hugging her purse. Her ash-blonde bob was frizzy from the pouring rain, and her eyes red behind her oval glasses. I slowly walked over to kiss her cheeks, my rain boots squeaking with each step. When I wrapped my arms around her, she seemed smaller than usual; I felt the bones of her ribcage with my fingers through her sweater. Neither of us spoke. I looked at my father lying in his hospital bed. The loose top of his light blue gown exposed his collar bones. I'd never seen him sick before, not even with a cold. Had I ever seen him laying down? He was always on his feet, fixing something around the house that wasn't broken.

A blood clot unknowingly lodged in his carotid artery on the left side of his neck had broken loose and made its way up his brainstem, blocking blood flow to a quarter of his brain. The part that controlled his ability to speak, write, and move his right arm and leg was atrophying. He had been transferred from their local hospital in the suburbs to Hôpital Notre-Dame in Montreal, which specialized in stroke treatment. I rushed from my nearby apartment to meet them.

As I approached him, I forcefully swallowed. Papa looked at me with an expression I had never seen on his face before: fear. I'd perceived only two other expressions from him, contentedness and anger. He raised his left arm and opened his palm. I put my hand in his and he squeezed tightly. We had not held hands—or hugged—in years.

"Come lay down on your pillow," my dad said, tapping his stomach. "Inspector Gadget is about to start."

I kicked my lion slippers off, jumped on the couch, and laid my head on his round, cushy belly. When I was a young child, papa and I watched cartoons together every Sunday morning—his only day off from the Kraft Foods plant—while maman and my older sister slept in. Inspector Gadget was our favorite.

I laid on my side across the middle seat of our pink corduroy sofa, my head on papa's lap, facing the TV. He wore a white tee-shirt and blue and gray plaid pajama pants, his legs crossed on the opened recliner. He rubbed his leather slippers together, as he always mindlessly did while watching TV: *swoosh, swoosh, swoosh.* I twisted around and looked up at him.

"Can we go get Egg McMuffins after?" I asked. "Please?"

"Okay. But just this one time," he said, pulling at my nose. He always said that.

"Yes! *Merci papa!*" I ran my finger on the cartilage bump on his thin nose. I inherited it—and hated it most of my life. Then I combed his thick mustache with my fingers. Papa couldn't grow a full beard, but he was proud of his mustache. It had tricolor hair: I could distinctly see red, brown, and blond hair. But I'd just noticed a new color.

"There are two white hairs in your mustache now," I said.

"No there isn't." He pulled my hand down.

I raised my index finger up. "*Un, deux...trois!*"

The following weekend, I found a mustache-less man in the living room when I woke up.

My mother and I sat alone in a beige corridor somewhere deep in the hospital basement, next to the *Staff Only* double doors separating us from my father. There were no chairs, only stone blue stadium-style seats mounted to the wall that we pulled down. My back rested on the cold cement wall. The dim overhead lights set a strange yellow glare onto the staff's white coats. I rubbed the palms of my hands together and slid my fingers in between my knees to get warm. How could a hospital be kept this cold? A nurse walked by and we asked for blankets. We heard each of his steps echo down the empty corridor. An hour before, the neurologist had stood by the foot of my father's bed, both hands in her pockets, and calmly told us there was a fifty percent chance he'd die on the operating table.

My mother quietly sobbed. Her face was brittle, but I'd rarely seen it break. Her head bowed down, slowly floating above her slouched shoulders.

"This isn't happening," she whispered. "It isn't real."

We both faced the wall in front of us, our shoulders touching to keep warm under the shared blanket.

"Do you..." I paused, unsure if I should keep my unaskable question to myself. "Do you regret not leaving him? All you do is fight."

Her answer was punctuated by her sobs. "No that's the thing. We were... things were better. We'd been laughing a lot together lately."

I was sad; twenty-one years in and they had finally gotten their marriage to a good place. My moving out surely helped.

Growing up, a lot of my parents' fights had centered around me. When I stayed up, reading in bed until two in the morning, I would get in trouble with papa if he woke up and saw light coming from my room.

"What do you want me to say?" I overheard maman tell him once. "She wakes up in time for school and has good grades. Just let her read."

When years later I asked maman how come papa became more permissive in my teens, she said he got frustrated and said "Fine. *You* do the parenting, I'll step back."

When I was twelve, on a family vacation to Charlevoix (one of the two trips we ever took), I designated myself as the photographer, enthusiastically cranking the film roll of my disposable camera in between shots. I asked to take a photo of my parents in the living room of our rental log cabin.

Papa pulled his arm around maman. "Let's kiss for the picture," he said. I rarely saw my parents be physically affectionate with one another. I quickly took the picture, the desire to look away tingling throughout my body. I found this picture again, years later, in a pile of Walmart Photo Center envelopes. In it, papa is leaned in, pressing his lips on maman's, eyes closed. Maman is standing straight, stiffly, her lips barely pursed, her eyes half open.

The neurologist calmly strode out of the operating room, the double doors swinging behind her. She was short and her white coat hung mid-calf.

"We were unable to move forward with the procedure," she said. "The walls of his artery appear to have merged. If we attempt to manually remove the clot, we would break his artery, which would be fatal. I'm sorry."

I looked down at the neurologist's black non-slip sneakers.

"We'll stabilize him," she continued, "but some of his organs may fail in the next few days."

My mother nodded faintly while the neurologist explained that my father may stop breathing, or his heart may stop beating. She asked us if we wanted them to resuscitate. My mother picked up the blanket that had fallen on the floor when we'd stood up.

"To be clear," the doctor said, "even if we can keep him alive, it's likely he won't ever walk or talk again, and we can't know if he will retain many of his faculties."

My mother looked at me. I felt lightheaded, everything went white. My eyes were still dry. Empty. I don't know what I said or didn't say. She told the doctor to let him go, if it came to that. He was fifty-one years old.

Maybe we sat back down in that corridor, maybe we were sent back to a room filled with beeping machines and color-coded wires. Maybe it was three in the morning, maybe it was noon. My thoughts went to my sister—technically my half-sister, eight years my elder—whom we had not yet called. She had lost her own father when she was eleven years old, just a few years after my mother divorced him. My sister was about to lose the man who raised her through her teens; my mother was about to lose another man she'd made a child with, and see her second kid become fatherless.

In fifth grade, maman parked in our driveway after picking me up from school and I rushed out of the car. I entered through the kitchen and vigorously closed the door behind me, the red slats of the blinds slamming against the door window.

I laid my math test on the white laminate table, in front of papa, and straightened the sheet with my flat hand; I'd held it the whole way home. Papa wore his dark blue work pants, his matching button up hung on the back of his chair.

"Bravo!" maman exclaimed as she entered the kitchen and placed her purse on the counter by the door.

"If you mastered 99% of the content," papa said, "you should have been able to get that last 1% correct." He took a pen out of his work shirt on the back rest.

"Look, it's easy," he said, drawing a line under my response.

"It's the best score of the class!" I said, irritated. "*So what* if I lost one point?"

"Hey, watch your attitude. The things my father would have done to me if I'd have talked back like you do."

I didn't remember my grandfather, a Montreal cop of Italian descent who died of a heart attack when I was three years old. The only thing I knew about him was that he refused to take his heart meds and that his punishment of choice for his children was belt lashes. Papa constantly reminded me that it was a privilege that I never received physical punishment for my fiery temper—which I took after him.

But I had yet to learn to shut my mouth, "I'm not talking back—"

"Hey!" His voice got louder. "What did I say?" The legs of his chair screeched on the white linoleum.

"I'm sorry," I said mechanically. "I'll do better next time."

"I know you will. Now give me a kiss," he said, tapping his cheek with his index finger.

I hated having to kiss him after an argument.

I walked to my room and heard maman ask him, in a low voice, "Couldn't you have taken a second to congratulate her on the test?"

I didn't distinguish the words in papa's reply, I just heard his familiar impatient tone.

My mother and I took turns spending the night shift on a blue vinyl chair with wooden arms by my father's hospital bed. The machines beeped every few minutes. A never-ending series of long and aggressive squeals. At night, everything in the room was a shade of washed-out green. My mother and I slept there for weeks, until a nurse finally convinced us that we wouldn't be of any help to him if we didn't properly rest.

We waited for a death that never came. It took months, but eventually, my father regained control of his basic functions; his brain figured out a new path to tell his bladder to empty when it was full and his throat muscles how to swallow.

Maman and I sat on the edge of our patio in the backyard. I was nine or ten, maybe older, but no more than 12, because it was in our first house, the cozy carpeted one with pink walls and a crawl space that served as my *cachette*. Maman was telling me something bad about papa. Perhaps that they fought all the time, that he was always angry at her. She might have been tearing up, her breath shaky while she took a drag of her cigarette.

It was new for me to see maman smoke. I'd recently seen a pack of red Du Maurier on the kitchen table and asked whose it was. There was a picture of a charred lung next to a healthy one on it; a new Canadian law. "It's mine," maman said. I looked at her, then at papa. I thought they were joking. "I've always smoked at the office," she said. "But now I'll smoke here too. Outside." I could sense when it was tense between my parents. It was rare to see maman stick with a decision that didn't make papa happy.

On the patio that day, I asked maman why she wouldn't divorce papa if it was that bad. Yes, she must have been crying for me to ask that question.

"He said he would hire the best lawyer and fight for your custody," she replied. "He knows I can't afford to hire someone good."

While my father was far from rich, his paycheck—which included overtime he did every Saturday paid at time and a half—was a lot more than what my mother was paid as a secretary.

"Well, I'll say that I want to live with you," I said.

Was this the beginning of the rupture in my relationship with my father? Or did my mother plant a seed that would later fuel my teenage reactiveness to anything he said and did? Was this the only seed she planted? Whether she'd done this knowingly or unknowingly out of fear of not being able to make it on her own, she'd drawn a line in the sand and asked whose side I would be on.

Over the following years, I lost grasp of the memories that made my father a human parent with flaws *and* qualities; I forgot about all the time he spent in the garage with me, helping me build contraptions I drew out of my imagination, like a water balloon catapult; I forgot the summer morning we biked to the park at five because I wanted to watch the sunrise over PB&J sandwiches (something my mother wouldn't have done). I forgot he *did* occasionally show pride, like when he browsed the comprehensive website I built on my own for a 10th grade history class project and asked me to teach him basic HTML. I complained he judged me with too harsh standards, always focusing on what I could have done better. Had I done the same with him?

My father moved to a long-term rehab center. His right arm remained paralyzed and his right leg gained limited mobility, not enough to walk properly. Despite hours of speech therapy, he never spoke again. He developed a wide range of facial expressions and intonations I had never seen before, and made noises in a voice that wasn't his. As if a stranger was uttering curious sounds from somewhere inside of him.

We were fifteen, tipsy, and Joannie's parents were out of town for the weekend. My father had insisted I stay home, but maman argued my case, saying I was responsible and my friends were too. She even gave her blessing to my older sister to buy me a six-pack of *Tornade*, a strong malt beer that tasted like lemonade. My father didn't know about that part.

It was a slumber party of three, but our other friend was asleep. Joannie and I faced each other on a plush loveseat, each resting our back on an armrest.

"Kiss me," Joannie said, out of the blue. "Just to try. I want to know if I'm good. With my tongue I mean."

I was astonished that Joannie would ask me something like this. After three years of weeknight phone calls and weekend movie nights, she'd still get stiff when we hugged hello and good-bye. She wasn't one of the girlfriends I'd fantasized about kissing before, but I leaned in and pressed my lips on hers without hesitation. Our tongues touched.

"Was that good?" she asked.

"Very good," I replied. I was relieved my braces didn't hit her teeth.

"Really?" she said, her round eyes wide open. Her naturally long eyelashes stretched above her upper eyelid and her green eyes glistened in the dimmed lighting. "Let's try again."

This time, I ran my fingers in her red curls and kissed her deeper.

Her lips on my neck, her fingernails in my skin. Our pajamas on the floor. My body acted with an intuition I didn't know I had.

"Does that feel good?" I asked, my fingers in her folds. "Yes," she replied, pulling my face in with both hands for a kiss.

The next morning, we woke up on a blow-up mattress on the floor of the windowless basement. My mouth was pasty and the top of my head felt like it was made out of lead. The mattress had gone soft during the night, and my tailbone touched the floor. I rolled around to shift my weight to my hip.

"I didn't expect things to end like that last night," I told Joannie, smiling.

"Never," she said with disgust, "*ever*, mention this again. This *never* happened. We were drunk, that's all."

"Oh, yeah. Of course… Obviously!" I turned my face away, looked up at the stucco ceiling and opened my eyes wide, fighting to keep them dry.

I focused on the mountain of logistical work that needed to be done to keep our family afloat. My sister had eighteen first graders to take care of on weekdays and two toddlers at home. My mother had been pushed out of the role of wife and forced into the role of caretaker. I took on the responsibility of caretaking for my mother. I didn't feel a dad-shaped hole in my life. All I felt was the burden of the pain that my mother was in.

I spent hours on the phone with insurance providers, pretending to be my mother, trying to understand how to access short-term and long-term disability pay. I worked with the financial aid services at my university to get a small scholarship and a deferred payment plan for the rest of my tuition fees that year.

My father always dreamed of living by the water. When I'd just turned fourteen, he became obsessed with real estate listings for properties we couldn't afford. I liked house hunting too, so I sat with him behind the bulky computer monitor at the formica corner desk in our basement laundry room. We patiently listened to the buzzing and high-pitched screeches that our modem emitted while initiating the internet connection that kept our phone line busy. Property addresses were not publicly posted then, so we'd print a few listings and scour the neighborhoods they were in, driving slowly. When we recognized one, we'd high-five and roll down the window to observe more closely.

One night we found a house for sale that was half-finished. There was no sink in the bathroom, the stairs were shaky and made out of two-by-fours, flooring was missing in some rooms. But it had a river running through the large backyard. The couple who designed and started building the house lived in it unfinished for over a decade before getting a divorce and putting it on the market. Because of all the work we'd have to do, the asking price was within range of what we could afford. My father and I loved a project, and this house was walking distance from my high school and would save me an hour-long bus ride. My mother did not want to move and disliked that for once, I was on my father's side. My sister didn't like the new house either, but now that she was at University she only lived with us on weekends. Eventually my mother caved. We moved on a cold December day.

The L'Assomption River was one of the most polluted watercourses of the entire province, but it didn't matter to my father and me that the water was brown. It was pretty to look at, especially frozen in the winter, and it felt luxurious to see it behind our yard. My father worked on that house for ten years, every inch of it. During the first few months, I helped him carry heavy boxes of tiles to the bathroom upstairs, and he showed me how to fish new wires for electric outlets and install new dimmers. It's the only time I remember spending with him in my teens.

After a few months at the rehab center, my father was able to move back home. On days my mother worked, the government covered an at-home aid. His comprehension skills were still mostly intact, so conversations with him became a complicated game of charades and Pictionary. While he couldn't write words or learn sign language, he could draw and mime with his left hand, and express himself non-verbally.

Numbers stuck though. He started drawing numbers in the air with his index finger to refer to people by their ages: 83 meant my grandmother, 60 his older sister. Once, he managed to ask me if I had a retirement fund with my new teaching job by writing "65" and a dollar sign.

This new normal felt stable, and so after graduation I moved to Nova Scotia for work, and a year later to New York City for grad school. I visited my parents four to five times a year, and my mother visited three times a year. New York City was an escape for her, an excuse to take a vacation from her caregiving duties.

"Papa," I said, "how can you say you'll vote for Stephen Harper, when he's against gay marriage?"

On the TV behind the couch that separated our counter height dining table and the living room area in our new house, Stephen Harper—the Conservative Party leader—gave a speech in French, rolling his Rs with the tip of his tongue. He reminded me of a creepy plastic doll, with his blue hooded eyes and tight smile.

"That doesn't bother me," papa replied.

"Maybe some of my friends are gay, you don't even know."

Maman gestured to let it go. *Just buy peace and keep your thoughts to yourself,* she'd often tell me. She'd also told me that she always told papa she voted the same as him, because he believed a family should vote together, but she often cast her ballot for a different candidate.

"What would you do if I brought a girl home and introduced her as my girlfriend?" I asked him, clenching my toes around the footrest of my chair.

"Well that would never happen," he said, putting his fork down and folding his hands in front of his plate, looking straight at the TV. "Because that's not how I raised you." After a long silence, he added: "Fifteen is too young to date anyway."

I pushed my fork through a piece of over-cooked carrot on my plate.

My father gesticulated with his left hand, pointed to my mom, then pointed to my sister. "Ma– No–," he said, enunciating his M and his N deliberately, contorting his mouth. Those were the two syllables he always produced repeatedly when he was trying extra hard to express something. I was visiting my parents, and my sister Mélissa, her husband, and her kids were sitting around the table with us.

"I went to Mélissa's school today," my mom repeated, speaking louder and slower. "to bring her car to the garage, and I brought it back before she was done teaching. What don't you understand about that?"

He moaned loudly, closed his fist and waved it left and right, as if he was moving a steering wheel, pointed to my mother, then to my sister again, his movements getting jerkier.

"You wonder where mom's car was?" my sister asked gently. "She left her car in my school's parking lot while she brought mine to the garage."

My father shook his head and groaned in frustration. He unlocked his wheel and moved his chair back a few inches before locking the wheel again. His left heel bounced up and down on the floor. He raised his hand again, and rubbed his thumb and index finger in the air, looking around the table with pleading eyes.

"You want to know how much it cost for the oil change?" my sister's husband asked.

My father waved his hand in my brother-in-law's direction to signify *no, you're going in the wrong direction,* and exhaled loudly.

Knowing my father, and knowing the kinds of things that have always preoccupied him in life, I decided to try something different. "You want to know if mom is covered by insurance when driving Mélissa's car?"

My father's face lit up, he vigorously pointed to me, let out a long joyful "aaaaah!" and started laughing. The whole family erupted in *yays*, claps and fist raises, cheering me as if I'd won a game show prize.

"Yes." My mom said. "Yes, my insurance covers when I drive other people's cars." My father let out a long sigh and looked at the floor, his energy reserve visibly depleted. I looked around the table, at the smiles on everyone's faces. The labor of conversing with my dad was sometimes tensed, sad, traumatic even. But this time, we made light of the fact that in some ways, my father hadn't changed at all.

I pulled a giant blueberry muffin out of a Costco tray and the thin plastic cover crackled when I pressed it shut.

"Alex," I heard maman's voice coming from the dining room. "Come sit for a minute when you're done."

Maman and papa sat next to each other, on the same side of the table, their back to the windows overlooking the tall pine tree. It wasn't their usual seats.

"Sit," maman said, pointing to the chair in front of them.

Papa slid his fingers in his fine brown hair, and looked at

maman. My temples pulsed like they did when I sensed I was in trouble. It was the winter of my ninth grade.

"We're separating," Maman said with a low voice.

I relaxed my thighs on the chair. I wasn't surprised. "This makes sense," I said. "You constantly fight. It'll be better." I broke my muffin in half with my fingers.

Papa's arms remained folded on his round belly. He didn't speak. Even though I knew this wasn't his choice, his eyebrows were relaxed, and his eyes dull.

Maman signed a lease for an apartment a couple of weeks later, and started painting the walls, getting ready to officially move out. The image of what the future might look like started sinking in. Would they split custody of me fifty-fifty, and have me spend entire weeks, alone, at papa's? I imagined what seven silent dinners in a row might feel like.

One cold afternoon that winter—the time of year when it gets dark at four—there were no lights on in the house when I came home after school. I worried instantly. Papa was always home before me. I usually found him doing his daily after-work round around the house: inspecting the house exterior, shoveling emergency paths or picking up leaves out of the gutters downspouts, pruning trees or shaking snow off branches. Or, I'd find him inside for his daily Swiffer round of the entire house, listening to *Cité Rock-Détente*, which I would have described as a soft "dad rock" radio station.

When I walked into the empty house that afternoon, I tried to put myself in his shoes for the first time. He didn't have hobbies outside of working on the house. He never went out with friends or colleagues after work. He didn't play sports. All he had was work and us. He must have known I was dying to move into my maman's apartment and never set foot in his house again. What was left for him? An image of his car crashed in a ditch on the side of the highway flashed in my brain.

When he finally arrived home two hours later, I rushed down the stairs and asked him where he had been. I stood a few steps above the entryway.

He began taking his boots off by the front door. He confused my worried tone for an aggressive one. "What do you care?" he said, his upper lip curled up. "You talk to me as if I was worthless. *Un moins que rien.*" I heard the tears he was holding back. I saw the despair and sadness in his eyes. It was unfamiliar to see his features rearrange to convey what was happening inside him.

"It's not true," I said, "I care. I was worried you had an accident or something." I didn't know what to do with my guilt, or how to be there for him, so I went back to my room.

Maman never moved out in the end. Part of me was mad, and part of me was relieved. My parents went back to whispering aggressively when I wasn't in the room, papa and I went back to ignoring each other. None of us ever talked about this one-month period of our lives again.

After my mother retired and lost her at-home aid, she became depressed and burnt out. Taking care of my father—and her mother, who'd become less independent—was draining. By then, I started exploring polyamory, and I often wondered what my mother's life could have been like had she had another companion to provide the kind of romance that my father no longer could. Or if my father had another partner who might share the daily care-giving burden with my mother.

When I was little, papa would say that, when I grew up, I was going to be his *bâton de vieillesse*, his *aging cane*—that instead of marrying, I would stay home and serve as his caretaker. I moved out the week after I graduated high school.

After spending hours trying to assemble the cheap futon that would serve as a bed in my windowless bedroom in the first apart-ment I shared with five roommates, I gave up. There was only one person who could help. I swallowed my pride and picked up the phone.

I didn't remember the last time papa and I had been alone outside of the house. He only took thirty minutes to finish the assembly, but it felt like hours. The awkwardness was palpable. We weren't mad, we were just both visibly uncomfortable. He was a ghost from a different life showing up in my new life as a free eighteen-year-old.

That was the only time he visited my apartment.

Every time I arrived at my parents' apartment for a visit, my dad rolled in his wheelchair all the way to the front door and waited for me to get out of the elevator. When I came in, his smile was as wide as his entire face. He made a long high pitched sound. I gave him a series of quick kisses on the right cheek, then on the left. He pulled me closer with his left arm, and hugged me tightly. A very long hug. Often, he'd playfully refuse to let go. Sometimes I was the one who kept my embrace tight, and I'd jokingly say he'd have to roll me around the apartment all evening. We'd laugh, and then we'd let go.

During one of my summer visits, as I was about to make my morning coffee, his loud "uuuh" caught me off guard. I froze in front of the opened cupboard, mug in hand, my arm raised above my head.

"What?" I asked, looking behind my shoulder. My dad rolled closer, his left index finger pointing at my armpit. I had stopped shaving that summer, and I was wearing a tank top.

"You don't like my hairy armpits?" I asked. "I'll shave them if you let me shave yours."

He looked puzzled.

My mother, who observed the scene from a stool at the island, joined in. "Women do this nowadays," she said, "it's the new trend."

My dad shook his head and rolled away with a loud "tsss" as my mom and I chuckled.

After watching *Le Jardin Secret* (*The Secret Garden*, dubbed in French), I asked my parents to make a secret garden in our backyard. Maybe I was six, maybe I was nine. Maman didn't think our small suburban yard could fit a secret garden. But papa took my hand and brought me to the back corner, between the above ground pool with the inflatable whale and the cedar bushes along the edge of our property. "How about here?" he asked.

It wasn't grandiose like I'd imagined. It didn't have tall rock walls and vines. But together we cut the grass out of a square section and planted colorful flowers.

On a cold fall afternoon twelve years after my father's stroke, I walked around my farmhouse. I removed leaves from the gutter downspout, I scanned for leaks in our flat stone foundation, and I inspected the oil level in our furnace tank. A memory of my dad flashed behind my eyes, and a weight pressed down on my chest.

The week after, I pulled the shaggy beige carpet on the upstairs landing, and uncovered beautiful ten-inch-wide plank floors. They probably dated from 1860, the year the house was built. After I pulled the last carpet staple, I put my pliers down and sat at the top of the staircase to browse YouTube. I scrolled through a list of video thumbnails, each displaying a different handyperson teaching viewers how to refinish hardwood floors. Tears blurred my vision. Papa would have loved to teach me that.

# SCENES FROM A POLYAMOROUS COMING OUT ON THANKSGIVING:

A one-act play & personal essay by
Alex Alberto

## CHARACTERS

**Me** (they/she), White, a young looking 32. I'm in
jeans and a loose sleeveless button down that
is more femme than normal for me, but still
highlights my strong shoulders and biceps. I
speak fast and have a voice that is often loud,
but today it's softer, and pitched a little
higher, in an unconscious bid to keep everyone
calm.

**Don** (he/him), White, 42, my partner of six years.
Don is 6'3" and 240 lbs, and the hard muscles he
had when we met have softened, much has migrated
to an endearing middle-aged paunch. He's wearing
a green plaid shirt and jeans that play well
with his blue eyes and gray beard.

**Aly** (she/her), White & Arab, 35, Don's partner of
three years; Recently our relationship has become romantic, but we are still figuring out
what that looks like for us (and asking ourselves big philosophical questions over salted
dark chocolate like "what is romantic love?").
She's wearing a tan sweater over her black
dress. She's always put together, and her makeup
reminds me of some of Don's Southern family.
I've always thought she was more beautiful without it. Although her Texas accent is usually so
slight as to be imperceptible, today, she's
leaning into a drawl.

**Cheryl** (she/her) and **Jim** (he/him), White, mid
60s, Don's Southern parents and our houseguests
for the week. Cheryl is wearing an indigo velvet
tracksuit. She and I have grown close in the
past few years; especially since I spent a week
in her home caring for her after her open-heart
surgery. Jim wears a polo with a small Alabama
Crimson Tide logo on the left chest, tucked into
his jeans. He's light-skinned and freshly shaven
with full red hair brushed and maybe sprayed—
the Southern executive's casual attire.

### SCENE 1

*Thanksgiving, 6 p.m., at the*
*apartment Don and I share in*
*northern Manhattan. It is gray*

*outside, cold for Aly's Texan-*
*Egyptian skin but not for my*
*French-Canadian bones. On stools*
*around the white island in our*
*kitchen, I sit on the end. Don*
*sits on my right, and Aly is next*
*to him. Cheryl is to my left,*
*facing Don, and Jim next to her,*
*facing Aly. It's the first time*
*that Don's parents meet Aly. The*
*recessed lighting is aggressively*
*bright; I keep thinking we should*
*install dimmer switches. The*
*lights reflect off the men's fore-*
*heads when they look in certain*
*directions. Everyone is smiling*
*too much when it's their turn to*
*speak, and not enough when they*
*think attention is directed else-*
*where. I hide my uneasiness by fo-*
*cusing on stirring my butternut*
*squash soup and blowing on each*
*spoonful even though it's the*
*perfect temperature.*

CHERYL

So, Aly, what made you move to New
York?

ALY

I was a musician based in Austin. I

toured with people who lived in New
York or LA, and they were hitting
industry success because they had
managers and labels, so I decided to
move up here and get a manager.

                    CHERYL
Have you left music behind?

                     ALY
I have.

                    CHERYL
Are you sad about that?

                     ALY
            (shifting in her seat)
Mmm… No. I found another artistic
outlet that I love, creative non-
fiction. And I still play.

                     DON
            (with pride)
I saw her play a full show.

                     ME
It was a great show. Two years ago,
in a famous venue in the city.

            I'm making conversation, but also
            conveying to Cheryl that there is
            no rivalry between Aly and me, and
            our lives have been blended for a
            while.

## scenes from a polyamorous coming out

                    DON
          (to Cheryl)
You actually listened to her album
last night.

                    ALY
Did you subtly put it on? It's like…
what do they call it?

                    ME
Subliminal…

                    ALY
Neurolinguistic programming?

          Aly, Don, and I laugh. Jim chuck-
          les. I feign nonchalance as I walk
          the four feet from my stool to
          the sink behind Aly and Don to
          refill my water glass. Cheryl says
          nothing and takes a bite of the
          mashed potatoes Aly made—her
          mother's recipe. The secret is
          keeping the potato skin.

                    CHERYL
          (her tone is an octave more
          serious)
And can I ask where you met my son?

          Cheryl looks at Aly intently. When
          Cheryl looks at someone, it some-
          times feels like a display of

dominance. Her eyebrows are per-
petually raised, and her unblink-
ing gaze is accentuated by her
tattooed eyeliner.

Three weeks ago, Don and I
emailed a long letter to his parents to come out as polyamorous
and explain who Aly is. We also
wrote about my pansexuality (we
used the word "bisexual" for
them), and mentioned my breakup
with Cara nine months earlier. I
left my gender-queerness out because that part is still too tender. Don's parents wouldn't speak
about the letter until their ar-
rival, but accepted to meet Aly
without resistance.

ALY
(slightly uneasy)
Umm… We met online. Yeah.

ME
Just like how we met. Your son and
me.

I sometimes try to avoid saying
Don's first name, because Cheryl
has said multiple times that she

*named him DonALD. Plus, she loves*
*the emphasis on her ownership of*
*him; he was her son before he was*
*my husband.*

CHERYL

Where?

ALY

Online. On a dating site.

*Aly turns to Don and me.*

ALY

The same one that you two met on,
right?

ME

(*nodding*)

OkCupid.

DON

(*with his storytelling voice*)

So, we had our first date at a bar,
and neither of us drank, but where
are you gonna go? We hit it off
immediately. We're having a great
date. When she gets a text message.

ME

(*laughing*)

Oh, that's a great story.

95

                    DON

The text was from her other partner,
now her ex. He'd been stood up for a
date *he* was going on, and he was
feeling badly about that, and so he
wanted to meet–

                  CHERYL

So he joined y'all?

          *I can't tell if she is amused or*
          *mortified.*

                    ALY

I also thought they would get along.
They had a lot in common.

                    DON

Yeah. He's also a PhD. Researcher.
Health stuff.

                    ALY

Tall.

          *I laugh because it's a funny addi-*
          *tion, but also because I crave an*
          *outlet to release the tension in*
          *my body. The stiffness in my neck.*
          *The hard knots in my guts. The*
          *pulse in my throat.*

                  CHERYL
            (not laughing or smiling)
That's funny.

DON

We ended up having a nice time.

CHERYL

(turns to me)

And where were you at the time?

ME

I think I was probably just home.
By the time they met, it wasn't as
stressful when he went on dates. I
mean, it always takes a little time
to get comfortable with a new person,
but once they've been around it's…
It's fine. Or it's great, actually.

> Cheryl holds my gaze. I can't
> decipher any emotion or opinion
> about what I just said. My temples
> feel warm under her observation.

ME

(waving across the table,
hoping to magically dispel
the tension with my hand)

Then it's like this!

> Aly and I laugh in nervous uni-
> son. Jim takes large bites of the
> Southern-style creamy green bean
> casserole I made. Don and I don't
> eat meat, so I used vegan bacon,

*which Jim is pleasantly surprised by.*

CHERYL
(quieter)
You know… I'm just um…

*I didn't know her volume could be low. Like me, she is a loud talker. She looks up at the ceiling for a moment and shakes her head.*

CHERYL
I'm old. I think that back in the day I may have had more of an open mind but…
(she turns to Jim)
What's happened to us? Is it our age? Or is it our background?

JIM
All of the above.

CHERYL
I mean this is… I'm still trying here. To open up. And it's just…

*I hear pain and despair welling from deep within her. She IS try- ing. Her voice trembles with con- flict. For the first time, I imagine what it is to be her, to have grown up in the '60s and '70s*

*in rural Alabama. I feel her love
for us, for me, and her battle to
keep touch with it.*

DON
(tenderly)
There's no rush. You're doing great!
You're doing great.

ME
Yeah, this is perfect.

*I appreciate her questions. It
always makes me uneasy—like someone isn't interested in knowing
me—if they avoid talking about my
polyamory.*

ALY
(softly)
It's been lovely. We're not asking
you to change anything.

DON
You don't have to throw us a parade
or anything.

*Cheryl holds Don's gaze with a
cryptic facial expression.*

CHERYL
How about I bring a John Doe to our
house as my lover? Younger.

*I smile and one knot is released*
*from my twisted gut. She is back*
*to playfulness, although there is*
*still an undertone of uneasiness.*

DON

We'll be very supportive. Whatever
you want.

ALY

I haven't told my mom about being
poly yet. My older brother's gay, and
she has a hard time with that. But,
you know, I respect that she's devoted
to her value system, and that's one
of the things that we have in common.
We just have different values. But I'm
not asking her to change.

DON

All we're asking is for you to behave
a certain way with the people we
care about. Not change how you think
or feel about it.

CHERYL

(*dryly*)

Well, 'cause that's your wife.

*She purses her lips as she takes*
*a sip of her water, and places her*
*glass back on the table. When her*

*glass hits the marble tabletop,*
*the sound is louder than before.*
*She doesn't slam it so hard, but*
*she clearly isn't restraining her*
*movements anymore. What does she*
*mean? Because we are married, she*
*has no choice but to behave*
*nicely with me? For the first*
*time, I feel some disdain di-*
*rected at me.*

ALY

I want to backtrack what I said
about my mom's values. I think that
her values and mine are similar. We
both value kindness, and love. It's
just that it manifests differently.

*I'm impressed by how well Aly is*
*navigating this conversation, and*
*I love her more for it. Cheryl*
*glances at her wireless glucose*
*monitor, which is always by her*
*side. She developed diabetes after*
*her breast cancer treatment a*
*decade ago. Jim is sitting back*
*and listening, as he does in most*
*conversations.*

CHERYL

But in your mother's defense, when

you raise children, you want to
teach them the value system. You
envision what's best for them. And
you want THAT.

> She bites into "that." The last T
> resonates around the table. It
> bothers me that she says "the"
> value system. Not "her" value
> system.

DON
(nods slowly, cautiously)
Because you want your children to be
safe, happy, and cared for.

CHERYL
(her tone raises, she speaks
faster)
Well, you don't have any children
yet. But yes, you want that, and
then some. My point is that, at this
very moment in time around this
"love table," if I had magical pow-
ers, poof! I'd pop you back into a
baby again and start over.

> She quickly waves her flat hand
> towards her stomach. It looks like
> a spanking gesture. Don and I
> laugh. Heat rises up my neck.

# scenes from a polyamorous coming out

                    ALY

My mom feels the *exact* same way.
Every birthday she tells me the
story of the day of my birth and how
she wishes she could go back.

          *I laugh. Cheryl ignores Aly, eyes*
          *locked on Don.*

                  CHERYL

I just LOVE you.

          *Her tone says I'm angry at you.*

                    DON
          *(low and tender)*
You would have waved that magic wand
*before* you learned of our polyamory.
Literally every time you see me, you
tell me you wish I was a baby still.

          *Aly and I laugh while Cheryl di-*
          *gests what her son said.*

                  CHERYL

Well, that is fair.

                    DON

I know!

          *Don laughs. He has navigated slip-*
          *pery discussions with his mother*
          *from a young age, always on guard*

*for something that would set her off. He is an expert at it.*

CHERYL

But, what's it called? Po-ly-ma…?

DON

(a touch short)

Polyamory.

*She asked the same question yesterday, and it disappointed him that since receiving our coming out letter, she made no effort to research what polyamory is.*

ME

The prefix "poly" means "many", and "amory" comes from "amor," which means "love." So, it means "many loves."

DON

We can get you some books and stuff.

CHERYL

No thank you. And that's not being close minded—

DON

It is, but that's okay.

*Irritation peaks in his laughs.*

104

# scenes from a polyamorous coming out

                    CHERYL

Well, you know...

                     DON
          (dryly)
Don't worry about it. I get it.

                     JIM

Yeah, there are some things we will
accept, and some things we won't.

                    CHERYL

Thank you, Jimmy.

                     JIM

It doesn't mean that we won't love
you—

                    CHERYL

I'll never lose you over anything.

                     JIM

It doesn't mean that we won't love
you, okay? We're sitting right here
with y'all, and it's a testament to
that. But what you're doing? We
don't... we don't accept that.

              *Jim is a cathedral of reasonable-
              ness, a granite temple of loving
              the sinner and hating the sin. He
              probably would have been happy*

*never to have known about this,
or to have ignored it forever, but
now that it's out, he can't remain
neutral. His forearms are anchored
on the table on either side of his
plate. Jim is a man of few words,
but when he opens his mouth, he
commands attention. I'm hurt when
I hear this, and confused by his
definition of "acceptance."*

CHERYL

And that's not anything against
either one of these two.

JIM

No! Nothing to do with that.

CHERYL

We don't mean nothing heinous. But my
first response to all this was "you
don't have to be married." You know,
in my opinion, I'd rather you NOT be
married, and it goes back to my
scripture. It goes back to MY beliefs.

*I muster all the energy I can not
to feel like this is a direct
attack to me.*

DON

Mm-hmm.

> Don keeps his lips sealed. I can
> see his jaw starting to clench.
> He wants to do everything he can
> to keep the conversation from
> derailing and crashing into a
> ditch.

CHERYL

That's all it goes back to. Doesn't
even mean I don't love Alex, 'cause
she knows I love her, and,
    (to Aly)
I don't know you well enough to love
you yet.

ALY

It's okay.

> Aly's eyebrows are furrowed in an
> empathy mask, and she nods her
> understanding gently. Her voice is
> soft, maybe to wind things down.
> She doesn't take this personally.
> Her only goal going into this
> dinner was for Don's parents to
> not hate her.

CHERYL

We're being honest, right?

ALY

Of course.

entwined

CHERYL

I don't know you yet but I… I LOVE
her.

> She points to me. I hear love vi-
> brate in her voice. Cheryl started
> saying "I love you" months into my
> relationship with Don, which at
> first I found off-putting. In my
> family, we don't say I love you to
> each other often, and definitely
> not to in-laws. Don explained that
> it was a Southern thing. The way
> she said it, it never sounded au-
> thentic, it felt void of emotion.
> But as years passed, and our rela-
> tionship developed, her "love you's"
> became sincere. It took me a long
> time to be able to say it back and
> mean it.

ME
(to Cheryl, sincerely)
I love you too.

> Don relaxes his shoulders. I am
> relieved that we reached a moment
> of respite, and hopeful that we
> can turn this around by focusing
> on love.

DON

And honestly—

CHERYL
(*pleads loudly*)
But you don't have to be married!
You know, to be tied financially to
someone, when you want multiple
loves.

> *I feel a small needle piercing my*
> *stomach. Aly has been watching*
> *the discussion with patience and*
> *tenderness in her eyes.*

DON

You were clear about that.

> *Cheryl's already weak filter is*
> *gone. I never expected her to*
> *be so upset about our marriage.*
> *"Mom is very clannish," Don has*
> *always told me. And she had wel-*
> *comed me into her clan, but I*
> *now feel her trying to push me*
> *out of it.*

> *Cheryl worked hard to escape*
> *poverty and secure an upper-*
> *middle-class life, including over-*
> *coming a couple of major setbacks*

in her fifties. Don says Cheryl
has always been obsessed with her
estate and who inherits what
after she's gone, even during
periods in which they had little
to pass on.

CHERYL

I just don't understand how this is
even working.

Her eyes are dry, but I hear her
throat tighten.

DON
(slowly, calmly)
It's working very well for everyone.
I promise you. And I appreciate the
things you said about loving me, and
Alex, so I want to say back to you
that the reason that we opened up to
you is because—

CHERYL

You love us.

DON

We DO. And I want you to know her.

Don puts his hand on Aly's shoulder
and she looks at him, half-
smiling. He takes his e-cigarette
out of his pocket—his tool for

> *releasing tension—and holds it in*
> *his closed fist.*

                    DON
Because I love her and WE love her.
Forget the nature of our relation-
ship. You've loved Sarah Beth in the
past, and you don't know whether
I've slept with her or not. Right?

                  CHERYL
        (cautious)
Right.

> *He takes a long drag, then a sec-*
> *ond and third in the same breath.*
> *When he turns his head to blow*
> *the smoke down the hall, it's*
> *quick, like he's blowing out a*
> *candle with a sigh.*

> *Sarah Beth is a close friend of*
> *Don's from grad school. He is*
> *godfather to her children, and*
> *Cheryl has met her several times.*
> *She even mails gifts for Christ-*
> *mas sometimes.*

                    DON
You love Sarah Beth because she's
somebody I love. So… I want this to
be an expression of my love for you—

# entwined

CHERYL

(turns to Jim)

I feel like I'm in the sixties.

DON

Let me finish. I've told you this,
and I wanted you to meet Aly, because I respect you and I want you
to KNOW me.

CHERYL

You know, if you had been like this
before you brought Alex into our
life, then I would buy some of that.
But you were not introduced to that,
and it wasn't something that you
went out and looked for before you
met her.

> Don's lower jaw juts outward, a
> sign that he has now crossed over
> to anger. He does not release
> Cheryl's gaze. I look down at my
> plate. I hear "If you had been
> LIKE THIS," over and over. I cut a
> piece of the vegan turkey Welling-
> ton and dip it in mushroom gravy.

CHERYL

(retreating somewhat)

Or did you look for that? Tell me. I
don't know.

*She raises her palms in the air.*
*Don keeps his eyes drilled into*
*hers, and does not move a muscle.*
*The rest of us are stoic spectators.*

CHERYL

You're getting upset. Because we're
being open.

*Don shakes his head. He calculates*
*how much he should say, knowing*
*the wrong move will escalate into*
*something too familiar for him. I*
*move my eyes from Don to Aly, who*
*I find looking at me. I look down*
*as soon as our eyes meet. I know*
*I can't keep holding my tears if*
*we lock eyes. Don smacks his lips.*

DON

The notion that you're going to
"buy" something that I say...

*He pauses, carefully lays his fork*
*in his plate, and exhales.*

DON

I'm being honest with you. You don't
need to "buy" it.

*He speaks low and lets all his*
*frustration diffuse in the word*
*"buy."*

113

DON

But, I hear where you're coming
from. I get it. Doesn't surprise me.
It's consistent with what you've told
me in the past.

JIM

Yeah.

CHERYL

So you expected it then.

DON

(inhales)

I did.

> I didn't. The fact that they had
> not canceled their trip or ex-
> pressed concerns before their
> visit had given me hope.

CHERYL

(to Jim)

But he's disappointed.

> Don gets up, and puts his plate in
> the sink. He moves slowly and
> lightly. I stand up too, glad to
> move my body.

CHERYL

I do the dishes since y'all cooked.
It's tradition.

                    ME

Fine. We won't fight you.

> Jim laughs. I can't wait to excuse
> myself and flush my tears. We
> discuss dishwashing, whether
> Cheryl should be on her feet after
> a blood sugar crash earlier,
> whether she can mix the lemon and
> pecan pie leftovers in the same
> container. I hear our voices as
> echoes. With Cheryl set in the
> kitchen, I walk our long corridor
> towards the bathroom and exhale
> slowly, looking at my feet. I hear
> Cheryl talking.

                  CHERYL

Well, this was a different Thanksgiving, Jimmy.

                    JIM

It was.


                 **SCENE 2**

> I sit on the toilet lid and rest
> my forehead on my palms. I let
> tears flow down my cheeks, then
> down my neck to my collarbones
> under my shirt. I inhale through
> my nose and forcefully exhale

through tight lips, breaths vibrating with sobs.

When Don showed me the draft
letter to his parents, I told him
he should add that I proposed
polyamory to him on our first
date. Since I didn't technically
have another partner—and explaining my romantic connection
with Aly would be complicated—I
feared his mother would pity me.
How did I not know it would
backfire? When confronted with
her son living a life she disap-
proves of, of course she'd pin me
as the villain. But I never expected "You were not like this
before you brought Alex into our
lives."

I look at myself in the mirror
and decide I should wait two more
minutes so my red eyes don't be-
tray me.

I run my fingertips through the
short hair behind my right ear. I
have an undercut on that side, and
curly blond hair down to my ear on

*the left. It's a new haircut that makes me feel more like myself. Before dinner, Cheryl took a photo of Don and me on the couch. "I really like your hair in this picture," Cheryl said. "I'll text it to you." Her compliment filled me with joy. But my chest tightened when I saw that the picture she sent was from last year, when my hair was down to my shoulders.*

*Just when I am ready to come out of the bathroom, I hear a few gentle knocks.*

ALY

Alex? Are you okay?

*Hearing her question reopens the dam. I swiftly open the door and shake my head, my face crumbling with fresh tears. She enters the bathroom and closes the door behind her. She takes a quick step towards me, as if to catch me, tilting her head and lowering her shoulders, her whole body folding into a shape that could hold both our pain.*

117

entwined

ALY

Oh, honey.

*One of her hands rubs my back, the other strokes my hair.*

*I pull back from her embrace. She delicately pushes my hair away from my face. Her fingers brush my forehead and my temples, and I want to kiss her right then. The urge has never felt so strong and natural. But I know this is the wrong moment for our first kiss.*

ME

Please don't feel responsible for this. I don't regret coming out and inviting you to dinner one bit. I want you here. You're family.

*She pulls me back into her arms, and I close my eyes for a moment.*

ALY

I'm glad I'm here.

ME

And now we can share the daughter-in-law burden together!

*I laugh through my tears. Aly*

laughs with me and rubs my
shoulder.

***

*Around eight, Aly explains she has
to go home and walk Casino. She
thanks Cheryl and Jim for agree-
ing to meet her, says that they
didn't have to do that and she
appreciated it. Cheryl asks if she
can give her a Southern hug, and
Aly says yes. Don puts his coat on
to walk her down. I hug Aly again,
and as I pull back, she looks
straight into my eyes and says, "I
love you." We said the words before, but never so simply. "I love
you," I tell her.*

## SCENE 3
### (As told to me by Don)

*The next morning, Don enters the
kitchen barefoot, in his gray
boxers and black t-shirt from the
day before. His thin hair is flat
on his head. Cheryl and Jim sit on
the couch, looking at their
phones. I'm out on a walk in the
rain, to get space, to collect*

*myself and recharge my empathy*
*and patience for the remaining*
*four days.*

*Don opens the refrigerator and*
*takes out a bottle filled with*
*cold water. He slides it into the*
*SodaStream machine on the counter,*
*and presses the button to carbo-*
*nate it, then unscrews the bottle*
*and pours in a half cap of energy*
*drink syrup.*

CHERYL

Son, did you schedule the asbestos
testing for the Upstate farmhouse
before you move in?

*Don and I have an accepted*
*offer on a farm in the Western*
*Catskills that we are buying with*
*a close friend, but we haven't*
*closed yet.*

DON
    *(groggy)*
I don't know, but Alex is on top of
all that.

CHERYL

You should have made it a condition
in your offer.

                    DON
We'll get it all done, Mom. We're
adults, living our life, and we know
what we need to do.

                   CHERYL
Do you have a problem with me?

          *Don squints his eyes then opens
          them wider, takes a long swig of
          his energy drink.*

                    DON
I don't have a problem with our
conversation this morning, other
than I don't understand why it's so
urgent to talk about asbestos before
I'm caffeinated, but now that you
ask, I didn't like how you talked
about my wife yesterday. You know
she went and cried in the bathroom?

                   CHERYL
Oh, she's playing you like a fiddle,
son.

          *Don doesn't have time to react
          before she opens her mouth again.*

                   CHERYL
And a lesbian, to boot!

          *The way she slathers the word
          "lesbian" with disgust does it.*

                    121

Don slams his bottle on the island and the energy drink fizzes
up and runs over the rim. Without
Aly or me present, neither Don nor
Cheryl have the restraint they had
last night.

Later, when he tells me what
Cheryl said, her words stay in my
body for weeks, months. I had
expected her to struggle with our
polyamory, but I felt safe about
my queerness. Cheryl is close to
her gay cousin, and sometimes
sends me articles in support of
LGBTQ rights. Even though I've had
to fight to legitimize my bisexuality, my straight and cis-passing
privilege has shielded me from
overt hatred.

DON

Get the fuck out.

His voice is quiet at first. He
crosses the living room to tower
over her on our low sectional.

DON
(crescendo to screaming)
Get the fuck out. Get the fuck out!

*Cheryl stands up, and mumbles something. Don isn't listening. He's lost control of his volume, and the part of his brain that's planful about what he's saying. He's run out of energy to filter himself after the last 30 hours—and 42 years—with his mother. Cheryl storms through the kitchen, and down the corridor. Don is steps behind, still screaming.*

DON

As much effort as Alex puts into making sure that you're happy, that we visit more often, that we call you, you should be kissing the ground she walks on when you come here!

*Cheryl enters our bedroom, where they've been sleeping, and walks into the ensuite bathroom. Don tails her. She starts to pack her toiletries.*

DON

The next however many years it takes you to feel sorry for what you just said are going to suck for you.

## entwined

Because I think you know this, but
in this family I'M the one who looks
out for your feelings and shit.

*Here, I imagine Don's Southern
accent thickening, as it does when
he's angry. After fifteen years in
the Northeast, his accent is still
thick to New Yorkers, but nearly
absent to Southerners.*

*He stumps back to the living
room, sits on the couch, aggressively sucking on his e-cigarette.
He sees a text message from me on
his phone.*

*"I'm on my way back," I wrote.*

*"Don't come back," he answers. "I
kicked them out. I'll let you know
when they're gone."*

***

*I freeze in the middle of the
sidewalk, frowning down at the
screen, shocked. I immediately
know Don must have voiced his
anger about the comments his
mother made about me last night.
I drift into a coffee shop. I push*

a doughnut into my mouth, even
though I don't like sweets in the
morning, then send a screenshot
of Don's text to Aly. She's not up
yet. I feel guilty, because had I
not gone on that walk, maybe
everyone would have navigated the
tension with a minimal filter.

*** 

Ten minutes later, Cheryl passes
through the kitchen, slides her
shoes on, opens the door quietly,
and leaves without another word.
Don assumes that Jim urged her
not to speak. Jim has always been
a calming force in their family,
balancing out Cheryl's intensity.
He crosses the kitchen, pulling
their rollers behind him. He stops
near the door, looks at Don, who
is still fuming motionlessly on
the couch, staring straight ahead
at nothing. When Jim speaks, Don
turns his head toward him.

JIM
I'm so sick and tired of being stuck
in the middle of y'all two.

DON
(calmly, but firmly)
This is on you too, Dad. You're en-
abling her shit. Saying "we won't
ever accept what you're doing." I'm
pissed at you, too.

Jim nods, still gripping the suitcase handles.

DON
And just so it's clear, I will not
see or speak to her again until she
comes back with a sincere apology.

JIM
I know.

DON
And don't try to put this all on
Alex. This is MY life. This is who I
am. And I'm proud.

JIM
I know.

He leaves the apartment.

I've always known that Don would
show his teeth to anyone who
disrespected me, but I never expected this to be tested with his
mother. I feel both safe under

*Don's unconditional protection,
and vulnerable to Jim and Cheryl's
judgements. After finally earning
their respect, I am demoted, seen
as lesser for wanting multiple
partners, for being attracted to
all genders. I feel a familiar
shame-one that I spent the last
decade freeing myself from-
gripping me.*

<u>End of play</u>

# from beginner to seasoned polyamorist

## Bed

**Beginner.** When Don changes the sheets after having sex with the slender journalist who says she's open to non-monogamy but hasn't agreed to meet you yet, you insist that the duvet cover also needs to be washed. You don't want her smell in your bed.

*We didn't lay on top of it*, he says.

You consider this for a moment but it makes you imagine the journalist's flawless naked body and the arithmetic of their sex so you say it doesn't make a difference to you, you want a whole clean bed to sleep in. You pull the hood of his red Alabama Crimson Tide sweatshirt over your head because it's February and like in most prewar New York City buildings the radiator has only two modes, off or hell hot, and there is a furnace inside of Don's body so he can only sleep in a meat locker. You slide the duvet out of its charcoal cover, barely resist the impulse to inspect it for creamy spots, and toss it into the sheet pile on the floor.

**Intermediate.** You hate going down to the laundry room in the basement, the one that usually has a roach or two stuck on the corner glue trap, dying a slow death. From across the bed, you stop Don as he begins to unbutton the duvet cover. *You were right,* you say, *washing the sheets is enough.* He asks if you're sure, which you appreciate because you know how much he hates making the duvet fit neatly into the corners of its sleeve.

A couple of months or years later you decide that changing the pillowcases is enough because when you think about it, it's the only *truly* intimate part of the bed.

**Seasoned.** Your phone dings as you're about to strip the sheets so you pick it up from the nightstand. It's an email from your boss—you should really turn off those notifications—and you look to the bed and you look at your phone and you look to the bed and *fuck it.* You kind of even like that when you fall asleep to the faint smell of lavender, you will be reminded that Bridget is in your life.

## Sex

**Beginner.** Any time you go anywhere, you look for opportunities to explore new fantasies. When you accompany Don to New Orleans for a conference, you find a sex club. At first, you're turned off by the dance poles and the loud electronic music. But you ascend the narrow staircase, Don behind you, and you find a candlelit library. There are floor-to-ceiling bookcases filled with hardcover books stripped of their jackets and it smells like rosewood. Four naked bodies are piled on a brown leather couch, moving together in a blob of moans and sweat. You and Don sit on a loveseat in front of them, and a stunning brunette draped in an indigo velvet dress that lifts her naked breasts as if on a display shelf asks if she can join you, sits next to you, says *it's my first time in a place like this and I want him to watch,* waves to a lanky person sipping on a plastic cup in the corner. You kiss her and rub her velvety thigh, and she kisses Don, and Don kisses you, and you watch the sticky blob of bodies in front of you and realize you're about to become one, too.

**Intermediate.** You prioritize intimate sex with steady partners like Frank, who geeked out with you about Educational Technology tools on your first date at the tea house in Midtown. He held his palms together in between his knees, slightly hunched over the table. You were instantly seduced because he was tall and fit and this posture made him look vulnerable.

You go out to eat sometimes, but sex remains one of your main activities. Though not at sex parties. Ideally before 9 p.m., in your soft bed between your fancy silk sheets that you bought off a clearance shelf, after you've brushed your teeth and peed because if you don't pee right before and after sex you get a UTI. You roleplay together, something you've never done before, but with Frank it's not silly, it's hot to try on new cliché personas, like when you pretend to be his stepsibling and cuff him to your headboard.

**Seasoned.** You make sex secondary or even tertiary to your life. Not just with Don, even with new partners. You get to know someone deeply before it gets too physical. Going on first dates takes a lot out of you, but after you haven't dated anyone other than Don for over a year, you finally open Tinder. You moved to the country and there are no polyamorous profiles in a 5o-mile radius, but you luck out on the queer app Lex and start messaging with Cara, a dimpled hiking guide who likes to paint.

You speak with Cara on the phone for two hours sitting on a log near the chicken coop, and when you hang up you call Don immediately, giddy, and he tells you it's nice to see you this high on a new crush, it's been a long time.

You take frequent walks with Cara on the rail trail and watch the leaves change. Then she proposes a picnic by a small lake and brings a home-cooked quiche with a lard dough, delicate plates and silverware that she wrapped in tan cloth. You don't usually eat meat but you happily make an exception since it's homemade and local and her, and the way she arranges everything with affection on your yellow blanket makes you feel like a king. She reads aloud to you, a chapter from her favorite book, and adorably holds it with both hands joined together, thumbs at the bottom of the same page.

You decided together to court each other. Two months pass before you kiss, and you like this new pace, you like savoring your desire, like when you watch *Portrait d'une jeune femme en feu* laying in bed, and even though your shoulders are not touching, they are so close that you can feel the warmth of her body through your sleeve and any time she moves, a hint of sage or maybe mugwort ensorcells you. She stays over for the weekend while you're on your period and places her hand on your uterus, kisses your lips, your neck, your nipples that she freed from your shirt, and you come for long, slow seconds with your jeans still zipped on.

## When your partner is on a date

**Beginner.** If Don has a date, then you have to schedule one for yourself. Only suckers sit at home while their partners are out getting laid. Or falling in love. Don will probably fall in love, and there won't be enough left for you. You hate first online dates but your other partner lives in Europe and you can't spend the evening with him on Skype because he falls asleep at his keyboard by 7 p.m., before Don has even left for his date.

The fact that you can't spoon your Austrian boyfriend or scratch his shaved head makes the experience feel very uneven with Don's, whose date might end up taking her underwear off in the bathroom and put it in his sports coat pocket while sticking her tongue down his throat like last time.

So, you go on a date with a surgical resident and you sit on a small back patio framed by vines and string lights. For a moment you think *oh this is so cute, and he's cute too*, you may end up enjoying yourself, but your date speaks extremely loudly. You are usually the one speaking loudly but he beats you easy and you finally understand how people feel when they are annoyed that you're too loud. It's a small courtyard with only six tables and everyone keeps looking at you and any time you say anything he agrees with like *we need more positive models of non-monogamy in movies* or *the mushroom flatbread is delicious*, he replies with a high pitch *hell yeah!* that ricochets off the brick walls.

He replies like this not just once or thrice but probably ten times, and you excuse yourself to go to the bathroom in hopes that Don texted but when you pull your phone out of your bra you see there is no text waiting for you. You sit on the toilet. You text your friend about the incessant *hell yeahs*. You want to swear once again you won't meet any more cishet dudes but they are the only ones readily available on all of the apps on nights like tonight, when you most need a distraction.

**Intermediate.** You put long johns on under your nylon pants and run in Riverside Park and you're alone because not many New Yorkers run in the winter but you're a Québécoise and you love it.

After you take a long hot shower you open the family-size bag of salt and vinegar chips you bought for the occasion, and you look through the television watch list you prepared that includes all of the most comforting old shows like *Friends* and *Buffy the Vampire Slayer*. You skip any episode about breakups.

**Seasoned.** Thank god, a night to yourself. You pull your favorite sweatpants out of the bottom drawer, the ones with a series of holes in the crotch, you order a vegetarian combo for two from an Ethiopian restaurant, you put on the *Rainy NYC Coffee Shop Ambiance with Relaxing Jazz* playlist on Spotify, you finish reading a YA fantasy novel, you masturbate, but not in the cute way, in the careless way with your right hand down your sweatpants, your oversized hoodie full of chip crumbs raised to your chin, your left pinky finger gently rubbing your nipple and your index finger balancing your phone sideways just above your breast, watching the kind of porn that makes you feel embarrassed the second after you climax and you're asleep before Don's date is over.

## After a date

**Beginner.** On the 1 train on your way home from a date with a social worker, you take your phone out of your winter coat pocket, and open the notes app to write down the progression of the evening before you forget; it's late, but Don will want a play-by-play of the entire date.

— Talked about his work with high schoolers at risk of dropping out and how I used to run after-school programs in Montreal for just that

— He currently has a friends-with-benefits who lives on Long Island that he sees about once every two weeks

— He never had a monogamous relationship, or any committed relationship it seems and our no sleepover rule didn't bother him

— We kissed while sitting at the bar, good kiss, not too much tongue

— He asked if I wanted a "nightcap" at his place around the corner from the bar, I said yes

— Sex on his futon: me on top of him sitting, him eating me out from behind on all fours then fucking me but his hands were not on me so I turned and saw he was rubbing his nipples with both hands so I flipped around, laid him down, straddled him and made circles on his nipples with my thumbs and he came very quickly. He went down on me again and I finished.

— We cuddled for a minute but I wanted to get going and he said we should do this again and I said yes.

When you get home, Don meets you at the door, kisses you, says *welcome home.* You take a shower together, and he gently soaps your entire body, even washes your hair for you. It's how you both transition back into each other. You give him your report in bed, his arm wrapped around you, your back against his chest. He asks follow-up questions and when you're done, he says it seems like you had a good time but aren't overly excited. You're not. You say you may see him again but it's clear to you that it would be just for sex. Don kisses your temple, your cheek, and rubs your nipples through his Lucero t-shirt that you like to sleep in. This detailed reporting was long and exhausting, and you're well fucked already, but having sleepy sex with Don after a date is reassuring for him and you understand because you also feel more secure if you connect sexually after he's been with someone else.

**Intermediate.** You walk into the apartment on Sunday around 1pm, after you spent the night with a date, and find Don exactly as you expected: watching NFL Red Zone, sitting in his mid-century recliner, wearing nothing but his black boxer briefs, phone in hand, keeping an eye on his fantasy football lineups. On the side table next to him there are two empty cans of Fresca, a giant can of Red Bull, and leftover Mexican food. He mutes the TV, and you ask him how his day was.

*Far less interesting than yours I'm sure!* he replies. *Tell me about your date!*

You give him a quick summary of the date, you just omit the spankings and *I love you*'s because he didn't specifically ask.

**Seasoned.** In between two vegan sushi bites, you mention to Don that you went on a date at a swimming hole Upstate with someone you met on Lex last Sunday, and that this one may have promise.

*Yeah?* he says, *what does she do?*

You say she's a nanny and lives like fifteen minutes from the cabin.

*That's great!* he replies. *Do you know when you'll see her again?*

You say you'll go hiking next Sunday, he says he's excited for you and asks if you want to watch the next episode of Survivor.

## Personal items

**Beginner.** When you come back home after work and drop your computer bag in the bedroom, you notice that the bottle of lube is on Don's nightstand. He had a date last night. He took *your* black bottle of fancy lube out of the closet, put it on the nightstand, pressed on the dispensing pump with his thumb (which was probably coated with her juices), held his fingers (which were probably coated with her juices) on the pump opening to scoop the lube up, then was going to do the same thing with you today or someday soon without a second thought?

You buy a second bottle of lube. They are identical, so you put a strip of painter's tape around the one that's just for you and you write "A" with a black sharpie. You don't label the guest one, because you don't want Don's dates to know how anal you are.

You start thinking about the other intimate objects you don't want in contact with someone else: you move the plush blue towels that a friend gifted you to the bedroom wardrobe and leave the rugged white ones in the bathroom closet, the ones that are slightly too small. Those can be for Don's dates. You open the medicine cabinet, grab your Sensodyne toothpaste, and put it in the vanity under the sink.

**Intermediate.** You hear a ding coming from somewhere within your layers. You take a few steps off the trail in your snowshoes, stick your ski poles in the fresh snow, pull one glove off with your teeth, unzip your coat pocket, and get the phone.

Aly's flight to Texas was canceled, Don says, and her house sitter is already at her apartment for the week, so I told her she could go to our apt.

Aly has keys to the city apartment in case of emergencies, but this is the first time she actually needs to use them. You try to remember if you left anything personal or embarrassing out before you left to come Upstate with Don.

You text Aly to ask if she knows when they'll reschedule her flight, and she doesn't.

I don't have any winter clothes in my suitcase! she writes.

You feel bad for her, you get so irritated when your travel plans go awry. You tell her she can borrow a hat and scarf from the black canvas box in the top right corner of the entryway closet, and your black winter coat from the office closet. You also tell her she can go into your wardrobe and get anything she wants: socks, long sleeve t-shirt, long johns...

This may be the first time you'll actually be dressed for winter, you joke.

You've been telling her that she's dressing for winter like a Texan and that's why she hates the cold. There is no bad weather, only bad clothing.

**Seasoned.** You slide your toothbrush in your mouth, start brushing the side of your upper left molars, and something isn't right. The bristles feel rough against your gums. You pull the toothbrush out of your mouth and inspect it. The bamboo handle is slightly curvier than yours. You look up at the mason jar on the shelf and see your toothbrush standing in it next to Don's and Aly's. You realize you just used Arielle's toothbrush, Aly's partner who is visiting you Upstate for the weekend. You feel bad for a moment, you don't even really know Arielle, you met her for the first time yesterday and now you put a really intimate item of hers in your mouth. But also, isn't it weird that a guest would put their toothbrush in the toothbrush holder when they're here for two days instead of keeping it in their toiletry bag? But also, oh well.

You open the bathroom door to Arielle and Aly making tea in the kitchen.

*Arielle,* you say, *I used your toothbrush by mistake.*

Aly laughs, and says *ah yeah, I noticed the two bamboo toothbrushes in the jar earlier and wondered if that would happen and then walked away.*

You tell Arielle that you have brand new extra ones if she

wants, and she shrugs, says she's not worried about it, and you shrug, and you all laugh.

## Getting dumped

**Beginner.** When you match with Susie on Tinder, she says she is cool with polyamory. You really enjoy your two first dates. She always wears what could be called an "ugly Christmas sweater" but you find it quirky and adorable. She loves to talk about languages as much as you do, and you can even do it in French because she's fluent. And she likes the Québec vernacular and accent, doesn't shit on it like most people you meet, like Don's friend who asked you "how you Québécois could take one of the most beautiful languages in the world and make it sound so gross." The idea of developing intimacy in French in New York City makes you feel ecstatic.

On your third date, you sit in a room with a clear roof, and the sound of the fall rain combined with the smooth jazz in the background makes for a romantic soundtrack. After the server brings the check, she tells you that *finalement, après y avoir réfléchi,* she doesn't think polyamory is for her.

**Intermediate.** You and Don are both zoned out on your phones, reading the news, enjoying a slow morning in the cushy king size bed in his parents' guest bedroom in Atlanta. You're there for the week to help his mother recover from an open-heart surgery.

It's taken you a lot to keep your emotions under control. Seeing her in her hospital bed and hearing how she thought she was going to die when there were complications the day after her surgery reminded you of the time spent waiting for your father to die after his stroke. But you didn't want to make things harder for her, so you managed not to cry.

A text from Frank pops up at the top of your phone screen. You tap on it, looking forward to his response. You sent him a text last night suggesting days and times to get together after you're back in New York City.

> The couples therapist I see with my wife suggested that I take a break from seeing other people until our relationship is in a strong place again. For the next month we're doing therapy twice a week so this process can go as fast as possible.

Your eyes fill with water and your breath stammers. You've been seeing Frank for five months.

Don asks what's wrong. You show him the text. *That's fucked up*, Don says. *I'm sorry.*

This is when you realize you'll need to assess if someone's style of polyamory matches yours before you let yourself fall in love.

**Seasoned.** Catherine breaks up with you because she moves to Seattle. Elliot breaks up with you because they work late as a bartender and you don't drink and like to be in bed by nine. People break up for a variety of reasons that have nothing to do with polyamory.

## Compersion

**Beginner.** You're sitting on your red yoga mat in your living room, legs straight, holding your toes with your fingertips. An episode of *The Magicians* plays on your laptop on the floor in front of you. Doing stretches before bed helps you sleep better. You hear the FaceTime call tone so you hit the spacebar on your laptop and pick up your phone from the coffee table.

*Hi sweetheart!* Don says with a bright grin. He's wearing a navy sports coat over a light blue button down, and you can tell he shaved his cheekbones and trimmed his beard. The stripe of white hairs on the left side of his chin seems more pronounced now. You find him majestic, and you feel a mild jealousy wave from your bellybutton to your ears because he got all done up for someone else, but it dissipates quickly. He is more alert than he usually is on your FaceTime-before-bed sessions. He speaks louder, faster, he gestures with his free hand. *Tara came out to her dad!* Don has been dating her for a few weeks. She had never really thought about non-monogamy before, but after meeting Don, she very quickly came to the epiphany that this was who she was. She was *polyamorous*. Don says this to you with some sort of pride. He's excited to be on that journey with her. You think about how you are the one who invited *him* on this journey when you met, so you know how this feels. You're happy to finally see him experience this new relationship energy.

Is that what compersion is? When you started reading the books and they described compersion as "the opposite of jealousy," or "experiencing joy when seeing a partner happily involved with someone else," you figured it was a bit of a myth. Even if you *are* experiencing sympathetic joy for Don right now, you just can't imagine you'll be uplifted if he meets Tara's dad, goes on a trip with her, and falls *in love* love.

**Intermediate.** You hear Don's keys in the door, and you ask what he's doing home so early. You're working from home, sitting in front of your laptop at the small dining table in the living room.

*I left work early and went to Bridget's studio for a Pilates session,* he replies.

*You what?* you say, amused, and stand up to kiss him.

He must really be into Bridget, because you've never seen Don voluntarily do any type of physical activity other than tennis, especially not one that requires him to lay down on the floor.

Don plugs his e-cigarette in the charger on the extension cord next to the couch and sits. You lower the blinds halfway down because the sun is blazing in the living room at this hour. You sit next to him, and ask if he liked it.

*Actually, yeah. I enjoyed it a surprising amount. "Pilates Bridget" is a whole new side of Bridget that I never knew existed.*

He continues before you have time to ask a follow up question.

*It was like she was a different person in her studio–which is gorgeous, by the way; not huge, but spacious, with clean new equipment, in the middle of Union Square. We were the only people there, and she was finishing the books for the day, so she asked me to wait a minute— which was weird itself, when I think about it. She usually gives me all her attention. I sat on a machine in the studio, then she came out of the little office, gave me a peck on the lips, and started the tour. I don't know what Pilates studios are supposed to look like, but it seemed like an awesome one to me.*

It's rare that Don elaborates this much unprompted. He seems in awe, and you've never really seen him quite like that with any-one.

*So she pointed at the first machine and said, "get up there." It doesn't sound like a big thing the way I'm telling it, but Bridget has never given me a direct order without a smile and a "please," at the very least. I think I bristled, and made a joke about it, like "ok, I'll get up there." I expected her to laugh and say something like "sorry, still in coach mode," but she looked me in the eye, not even a smile, and nodded. Then she smacked my butt to hurry me up! The exercises were a lot more difficult than they looked. I made a lot of mistakes, in terms of my form, and she started using her hands to place my body how she wanted it. That's when it shifted for me.*

He pauses, takes his e-cigarette out of the charger and takes a long drag, followed by two quick ones. You're enjoying feeling Don's whole body buzzing as he's telling you all this. He seems younger for a moment, or less poised, experiencing the thrill of tapping into a new part of himself. He continues.

*And I realized: Damn, it's really sexy that my girlfriend is an expert on this thing that's new to me, and she's teaching me, and molding my movements in a way that no one ever has. It sort of made me wonder what it would be like if she were in charge outside the Pilates studio.*

You tell Don it's nice to see him full of adrenaline after this experience. You say that usually you're the one like this, talking and talking after a date and he laughs and squeezes your neck. You know the space he's describing well, when someone you respect and trust takes control of your body in a way that lets you exhale and tune into yourself, every one of your senses heightened. Don takes you there often. You've taken exes and lovers there often. You have no interest in taking Don there, so you feel no envy. You simply enjoy witnessing this new path of exploration opening for him, and you're glad that Bridget might lead him along.

**Seasoned.** *What time do you want to do breakfast today?* you text Aly. Arielle, Aly's partner who is visiting the farm, said she wanted to cook for everyone.

Aly writes that she's not sure, Arielle is still passed out, and sends a picture of Arielle in bed, on her back, under the balled up purple comforter, her short hair spiking in all directions. Casino is also asleep in the bed, laying on her side with her back pushed against Arielle and her paws dangling off the mattress. The sight of them together fills your heart with tenderness and you *aw* out loud. *Look at your babies!* you text back. You love that Aly shared this intimate picture with you.

*Alex*, she'd told you weeks earlier, *I'm really falling for her. The intensity, and the intimacy we have. I think about her all day.*

You feel no resentment hearing this statement. You know the kind of intensity she's talking about. You're happy she's getting a big scoop of it this week.

**Beginner, again.** You're in bed in the farmhouse, your phone laid face up on your bare stomach. A large fan oscillates in the corner of the room. You're in the middle of your daily bedtime conversation with Don; his voice comes out of the phone speaker. He's at the apartment in the city, and just came back from a sixth date. You tap your fingers on the hard cover book laid next to you on the bed. *You've been going to the city a lot more lately*, you say. *It's clear to me that it's because of your dates with Saga. And I love to see you excited about someone new since Aly, but I can't help but notice it affects my daily life, because it means you're away much more* *often. If you dated someone around here, you'd be going for a day and then coming back.* Saga was very upfront with Don when they met: she's worked very hard to build a community in New York City when she moved back after living abroad for fifteen years, and now she has it. She has her village, and her two kids love their school, so she won't be moving anywhere. That used to make you feel at ease, that someone had life circumstances that meant they would stay somewhat accessory to your and Don's life. But now, it's the opposite. You want to grow your family. You want your metamours to bring something to *your* life too. This has made it hard for you to feel untainted compersion when Don tells you about Saga. Even when he tells you she's obsessed with your writing and shares the videos of your public readings with her mother and her friends and she can't wait to meet you. *Well,* Don says, *we did talk about the possibility of her visiting the farm. It's not because she doesn't want to move up that she can't become a part of the extended family.* Why is it that you can't seem to feel happy about that? You used to love time apart from Don, space to miss him, space to come back to yourself and remember that you're independent. *Maybe once we have a larger family unit here at the farm,* you say, *it'll feel better for me. For now, when you're gone, the house is empty.*

## Disclosing

**Beginner.** Online, it's easy. Your profile describes your non-monogamy. On a Sunday morning, during brunch at the pub you work at while you're in grad school, you and your colleague chat while things are slow. One of your regulars walks over to the corner between the bar and the stack of extra chairs, where you're standing. He hands you his phone number on the back of his check. He isn't the first one to leave a number on a check, but he is the first one to hand it to you instead of leaving it on the table. You think about mentioning something about polyamory then, and how you've been seeing someone for a few months, but you don't.

On your walk by the water in Greenpoint, you think about mentioning something about polyamory, but you kiss him instead.

When he introduces you to his seven roommates who share a loft with him in Bushwick, you think about mentioning something about polyamory, but you figure it's better to wait until you're alone.

After five dates, you decide you're going to end things anyway, so you never mention anything at all.

**Intermediate.** You flirt for weeks with the wiry guy who wears thick round glasses and always arrives five minutes late to your Plant Science course at the New York Botanical Garden. When you're both by the water fountain filling your bottles during the break in the middle of the last class, he asks to exchange numbers to *maybe grab coffee sometime*, and he looks down at his blue sneakers, and you stop breathing for a second because you're smitten but also you have to tell him. You should tell him *now*.

So you blurt out that you're-polyamorous-and-polyamory-for-you-means-multiple-romantic-and-sexual-relationships-and-you-currently-have-one-partner-with-whom-you-spend-half-the-week-and-just-so-you're-clear-you're-not-looking-for-sex-though-sex-is-nice-of-course-but-not-the-focus-you-have-real-room-for-another-partner-in-your-life-now-sure-you-have-made-some-mistakes-in-the-past-but-you've-grown-and-know-what-you're-doing-more-or-less-and-you-would-love-to-go-on-a-date-if-all-of-that-is-okay-with-him-otherwise-friends-is-okay-too!

He says it's cool. You give him your phone and he types his number in, but he'll never reply to your text message.

**Seasoned.** This is how you're finally able to bring up poly-amory smoothly to new crushes:

Just kidding, this part may always feel tricky.

# queer en français

The first time I read the word *bigender* in a book, I instantly burst into tears. My full body shook, I couldn't breathe, I wailed on my couch for I don't know how long.

For most of my life, the only words about transness that I knew were *trans man*, and *trans woman*. Even if I was pretty sure I wasn't a man, I'd always been *dépaysé* in girlhood and womanhood. *Dépaysé*. The middle part of this word, *pays*, means *country*. Being *dé-pay-sé* means being "de-countried." It's the feeling of disorientation that you have when you find yourself in a country that is not your home. But the word is not just used for being in a foreign country, it's used to describe a feeling that you get when things around you feel unfamiliar. You feel uneasy—trying to understand what's around you, how things work, where you are, as you're navigating the world. It feels unmoored.

I've felt *dépaysé* my whole life. In my own culture. At home. At school. In my own body. I thought that I was failing at being a woman. That there was something wrong with me inside. *Bi-gender* was a mooring.

I eventually learned more words. *Non-binary. Genderqueer. Genderfluid. Gender non-conforming.* Maybe these words amassed to a country, a continent that I didn't know existed. The promised land that I would belong on, where I could be free. My true self.

I'd just turned twenty-four years old when I moved to the United States. My whole self-discovery journey happened in English. I processed emotions in English with friends and partners, I read books about polyamory, bisexuality and queerness in English, I even did therapy in English. I became a fully-formed adult and found my identity in my second language. I can't technically describe English as my native language since I wasn't fluent until I was sixteen, but English *is* the native language of my queerness.

I used to prefer the word *bisexual* as an identity label, because when I used *queer*, people assumed I meant *gay* or *lesbian*, and when I used *pansexual*, people's eyes became question marks. There was so much erasure of bisexuality—even within the limited LGBTQ+ representation—that I wanted a way to make it louder, more visible. I didn't want it to get absorbed by *queer*. But maybe I also clung to that term because it exists in French. The word *queer* doesn't. The rainbow letters in French stop at the T in LGBT. It makes sense: "queer" was once a derogatory word that was reclaimed by the English-speaking LGBTQ+ community. Its translation—*étrange* or *bizarre*—was never used as a slur in Québec or France. But describing myself as *queer* now feels more authentic to me, and it has for years. *Queer* feels like a loose cloak that allows me to grow, evolve, change shape. It gives room to my fluidity. It feels like it encompasses all the parts of me: my pansexuality, transness, polyamory. In more recent years, queer was borrowed from English and has entered the French lexicon, but it's not widely used. It's not a concept my mother would have known—which may explain the gulf I feel between my newfound authentic queer self and my French-Canadian culture and language. Each time I visit, speaking French with my parents, sister, and friends feels like expressing myself in a foreign language.

I used to agree with the common opinion that French is a richer language than English—I found French had more nuanced expressions, a wider vocabulary, and more complex sentence structures that allowed more creativity. But French is extremely gendered. In English, the gender of a person is only apparent when another person speaks about them in the third person. In French it's present even when speaking in the first person. For example, if I say "I am happy," I have to pick either the feminine form of the word happy, *heureuse*, or the masculine form, *heureux*. If I say that I'm a farmer, I have to pick whether I use the feminine version of farmer (*fermière*, with au audible R at the end), or the masculine version (*fermier*, the last R being silent). Even though a new gender-neutral pronoun was created, words and adjectives still have to be feminine or masculine. Some people have started to make up new words with gender-neutral endings, but there is such a large number of distinct gendered endings that memorizing new ones for every word would be a huge task. When English speakers say that it's hard for them to adopt *they* as a gender neutral pronoun, I am of the opinion that they are simply unwilling to try. It is a low barrier to entry. French speakers who complain of the struggles to speak in a gender neutral way aren't being difficult. It *is* difficult.

The masculine pronoun in French is *il*, and the feminine is *elle*. The new gender neutral pronoun is *iel*. But while I'd love to ask my French close ones to use it when referring to me, it still leaves all of the gendered nouns and adjectives. It still leaves me with deciding whether I want to use masculine or feminine words when describing myself, or alternating. The pronoun *iel* also doesn't roll off the tongue easy because of the way Québecois colloquially use contractions. In writing, it can be used easily, but not when speaking informally. I've considered asking people to still use *elle*, the feminine pronoun, when referring to me, but use masculine adjectives to offset it. It would require some mental gymnastics, though it feels attainable for anyone willing to try.

The fact that I can't speak in French without signaling gender pains me. I love that, in English, gender is less present in my conversations. But it recently occurred to me that I can turn this into an opportunity: When I speak in French, *I* get to indicate my gender. To have my gender affirmed in conversation, I don't have to wait for someone to describe me in the third person. I control my gender expression. I get to be creative with language in whatever way I want that day, that conversation, that *sentence*. I can choose to embrace my fluidity and move between masculine, feminine, and gender-neutral neologisms.

"Don't you feel lonely when you're not with Don?" my mother asked me. She sat on my low couch as I sat on the floor on my yoga mat, stretching after running the thirty-six blocks separating Don's apartment from mine.

"No," I replied, trying to grab my toes with my fingers. "I love having a few days a week to miss him and the space to be on my own."

"Well, you've always been very independent," she said.

I took a deep breath, my heart still pumping ten minutes after my run. I'd wanted to tell my mother I was polyamorous for a long time, but I felt like I needed more evidence first. I needed to have been with Don for long enough so that when she found out, she'd *have* to believe this was the right choice for us. That this was the road to happiness for me. That despite all of her doubts and questions, she'd have to admit that she'd never seen me happier.

I looked up at her on the couch while I was still stretching on the floor. I opened my mouth, closed it, then opened it again. "On our first date," I said, "Don and I were both very clear with non-negotiables. He said keeping separate living spaces was important to him. I hadn't thought about it before, but it actually made a lot of sense for *my* non-negotiable, which was that I wanted to continue dating other people."

She looked at me for a moment, her eyebrows furrowed. Then, with a small amused smile, she asked "Puis? Avez-vous continué?"

"Oui," I replied, "we're still dating other people today." I heard myself laugh nervously, glad that the sweat running down my red cheeks could be attributed to my run.

"Est-ce que je peux poser des questions?" she asked.

"Oh yeah," I said, "please ask as many questions as you want. I love when people ask questions. This is a big part of my life, and who I am, I don't want to feel like you're tiptoeing around it."

She asked if we met the people the other dated, and if we did out of town trips with them. I said yes to both, and explained that I considered Bridget, Don's girlfriend, family. In fact, when an apartment in my building was put on the market, I'd fantasized about Bridget moving in it.

"It's kind of like having a sister-in-law," I said.

My mom cocked her head and smiled. "Except that she sleeps with your husband," she said, and laughed. I laughed with her. "Well," she said, as if she had reached a conclusion, "I knew so many people in my office who had mistresses and lovers. It's a lot nicer to do it all in the open."

I pulled my knees to my chest and exhaled. I knew my mother would ultimately be accepting of my polyamory, but I had expected her to be awkward about it for a while at least. This was a relief.

"Have you dated anyone I know?" she asked.

I cleared my throat. "Hum, yes. Do you remember Kate?" Her eyes widened and she stared at me for long seconds. "We went to high school together," I added.

My mother shook her head, as if she'd just woken up from a trance, and quickly said "yes yes, the pianist. Of course I remember Kate."

I looked down and tugged at the edge of my yoga mat. I should have known that the queer part would be more uncomfortable for her. *Je suis bisexuelle*, I wanted to say, to make sure I was being clear, to make sure I was truly coming out about everything. But I couldn't utter the words.

"I've always liked Kate," she said.

Two years later, a few weeks after we told them we were polyamorous and that I was bisexual, Don's mother and step-father visited us for Thanksgiving. As I fished ground coffee out of the pantry, Don's mother asked me how my mother had responded.

"She took it very well," I replied, putting a few spoons of coffee into my French Press. "She said she always knew I was different, even from a young age."

While I was in the bathroom later, I heard Don's mother's voice carry through the hallway, talking to him. "Apparently Alex's mom always knew Alex was different, but you were not different. We didn't raise you *different*. You were a normal kid."

My heart sank. When my mother said the word *different*, it was filled with love. It made me feel like she'd always seen me, even if neither of us had the words or conscious understanding of who I was. That's how I thought Don's mother would hear it. But when she repeated *different*, it was filled with loathing.

When it began to feel natural for me to express myself in English, that ease caused me tremendous guilt. It was as if, by assimilating my thoughts and speech into the language of the English, I'd betrayed my Québécois heritage. French-Canadians fought empires and sacrificed opportunities for hundreds of years to preserve Québécois language and culture. In the mid-18th century, when France ceded Quebec to England, the British government implemented policies that threatened the French language and the Catholic religion. As it did in India, Africa, and the Caribbean, the British sought to assimilate French-Canadians as second-class citizens of the British empire through linguistic oppression. By the 1900's, English speakers far outnumbered French-Canadians, and they used their majority to pass laws (including compulsory military service) despite strenuous opposition in Québec.

During the 1960s, in a period of intense social and political change known as the Quiet Revolution, Québécois challenged the dominance of English-speaking institutions and asserted Québec's distinct identity. In 1977, the Quebec government passed the Charter of the French Language, which made it the official language of the province and the workplace, restricting the use of English in public signage and businesses.

Minority groups who have survived legal segregation and oppression rarely forget that it occurred, as much as the oppressors wish they would. French-Canadians know both sides, because Indigenous people were on the land when they arrived; we're both oppressor and the oppressed. Still, in Québec, when we talk about Canada, we mean English Canada. I've never called myself Canadian, except abroad. Even then, I say *French*-Canadian.

It's rare for Québécois to move out of the province—even to English Canada. Moving to the United States felt like moving to the belly of The Beast. I once heard my friend's dad refer to English as *la langue de l'ennemi*, the language of the enemy.

Almost all of my childhood friends still lived close to their parents and siblings, but there I was, an American *citizen*. That was bad enough—but now I also wrote my most intimate stories in English. La langue de l'ennemi.

It didn't occur to me for a long time that maybe building a life in English contributed to my survival.

I laid in bed perpendicular to Don, my head resting near his arm-pit, his arm wrapped around me. I was reading *The Family Outing* aloud, the pages illuminated by my red reading lamp. The rest of the room was pitch dark. Early in the book, Jessi Hempel ex-plained that throughout the story, she'd use he/him pronouns to describe her brother, and wouldn't use his dead name—even when talking about the time before he was out as trans. At first, she thought it would be hard to describe her brother as a child this way. But then she wrote:

> *"Something fundamental has changed for me as I've lived with Evan; I've refashioned that history. I've leaned into the emo-tional truth of it, and as I have, Evan has come clear. Who he was has emerged. Evan was a willful child, a kid who was al-ways self-possessed, who arrived everywhere fist first. He was stubborn and independent, uninterested in following other people's rules. As I describe—"*

The words got stuck in my throat. I closed my mouth and tried to control my incoming sobs and prevent my body from shaking. I'd been avoiding talking about my gender questioning with Don. For a moment I wanted to hide my emotion, but I knew he felt it. He was the one who had gently nudged me a few times, saying maybe I should spend some time interrogating my gender iden-tity. I'd been avoiding it for years, and while I could no longer ignore my turmoil, I didn't know how to bring him in. Normally he was part of all of my emotional processing and identity exca-vation, but this one felt difficult.

I put the book down on my stomach and gave into the tears.

Don put his palm on my forehead and kissed the top of my head while I cried quietly for several minutes.

"What does it say about you," I said when my sobs calmed, "if I'm not a woman?"

"What do you mean?" Don asked in my ear.

"You're straight. If I'm not a woman, what does it mean for our relationship?"

"Oh, cub," he replied, holding me tightly with his second arm. "Listen to me. There is *nothing* about that that would make me stop loving you. I love *you*. Not your gender or your genitalia. We are family, forever, no matter what."

I continued crying in Don's arms, and with each shoulder contraction that accompanied my sobs, I felt the tension release from my body.

A year after I started asking people to refer to me with they/them pronouns, I invited my mother to visit me the week that I was going to a ceremony for an arts grant I'd received. I'd be teaching memoir writing to the LGBTQ+ community in my rural county. I knew she would hear all my friends using *they* when talking about me, and that they would introduce me with that pronoun at the ceremony. I wasn't sure she even knew that "they" could be used as a gender-neutral pronoun, but I knew I wanted to continue being myself when she visited. I'd grown happy and comfortable, and if I wanted to receive her in my world, I needed her to know who I was. I wasn't worried that she would react negatively; but I was dreading having the conversation. My mind knew she'd love me no matter what, but my body was a ball of tangled knots. The night before the ceremony, Don, my mom and I sat around the table in our kitchen, finishing dinner. I spoke to her in French, even if Don wasn't fluent yet. He knew enough to hear keywords.

"I need to tell you something before the ceremony tomorrow. When they introduce me, they will not use *she* to talk about me. They will use *they*, which is a gender-neutral pronoun in English, because I am non-binary, meaning I don't identify as a woman, or a man." I spoke quickly, looking down at my spaghetti plate.

My mom nodded energetically. "Okay."

"When we have conversations in English with Don, or other people, I would like it if you tried to use *they*. It's okay if you mess up, I can imagine it will be harder because it's your second language, but all I need is for you to try. You don't need to change anything in French yet, because it's nearly impossible to speak in a gender-neutral way in French, and I haven't decided how I want to handle that."

Her face lit up. "Oh no there is something in French, I read it the other day!" She looked proud to be in the know, and my heart softened. I switched to English to allow Don into the conversation.

"Well, there is a pronoun, *iel*, spelled I-E-L, but the problem is with the nouns and adjectives."

"Oh, I see!" she said in English. "You should have told me a long time ago!"

Don jumped in. "For a long time, Alex did not want to think about their gender. They avoided it, because it was very emotional for them. And every time we talked about it, tears would run down their face."

My eyes watered and tears rolled down my cheeks, but my

mom and Don were looking at each other. I took a loud breath in, and Don turned to me.

"Just like this," he said.

My mom's eyes watered too. "It's okay baby," she said in English. "I love you. I will always love you."

I put my face into my palms and cried louder. Don pressed his hand on my shoulder. I stood up and walked around the table to my mom. I bent down to hug her.

"It's okay, baby," she repeated in English. "I love you."

# blockbuster tropes reimagined with polyamorous characters

### Love Triangle:
### *My Best Friend's Wedding*

**Original:** After having "one hot month," with Dermot Mulroney while they were in college, Julia Roberts gets restless and breaks up with him, but they remain best friends for the following decade. When Mulroney calls Roberts to tell her he's getting married to twenty-year-old Cameron Diaz, Roberts flies to Chicago days before the wedding to break them up.

**Reimagined:** Instead of being threatened by Diaz, Roberts is thrilled someone wants to follow her best friend and enduring flame around on his boring sports writing trips. Roberts has no interest in that; she's an independent woman who gets restless when tied down. At the lunch wedding party, Mulroney is the one who sings "I Say a Little Prayer" to Roberts and Diaz, leaning into his Virginian accent: "Forever, and never, we never will part, oh, how I love *y'all*, together, together, that's how it must be, to live without *y'all* would only mean heartbreak for meeeee." The end.

**See also:** Twilight, True Blood, Vampire Diaries, and Buffy the Vampire Slayer. Why choose between supernatural creatures?

## Fear of Commitment:
### *The Runaway Bride*

**Original:** A reporter (Richard Gere) is assigned to write a story about a woman (Julia Roberts) who has left three fiancés at the altar and is engaged for a fourth time. In his interviews, Gere asks each former fiancé how Roberts takes her eggs in the morning. One after the other, they reply "poached, just like me," and "scrambled, just like me." Gere tells Roberts this is indicative of how lost she was in her relationships, he proposes, and she finally says yes at the altar.

**Reimagined:** Gere goes to Small Town Middle of Nowhere to report on Roberts' singular love life: She has happy relationships with four partners. Solo-polyamory is what suits Roberts; she doesn't intend to merge her dish sets and sheets or open a joint bank account. She lives alone in her loft, where each partner has an individual drawer for the one day a week they visit. She still hits her punching bag regularly, but because she's a badass independent woman, not because she's lost without a husband and doesn't know why she can't say *I do*. When Gere asks her out, she gives him a chance and they go out for burgers and mechanical bull riding (it is a small town in a Hollywood movie, after all). But after dating for a few months, Gere still can't get the shared Google Calendar to sync on his phone and seeing other men's chest hair on the floor of the shower makes him feel insecure. He demands she break up with her two boyfriends, and graciously offers that she can continue seeing her two girlfriends, as long as they keep it to a strictly sexual relationship and let him watch from time to time. He argues that Roberts' polyamory is just a phase and that the fact she takes her eggs in a different style with each partner means she doesn't know who she is and hasn't found her one-and-only. Roberts laughs in his face and says she likes to eat whatever the fuck strikes her fancy. They break up and all of her partners come over and bring pints of cookie dough ice cream. The end.

**See also:** Pretty Woman, Eat Pray Love, Notting Hill. Polyamory would end Julia Roberts' career.

## The Jaded Lover's Violent Revenge:
### *Fatal Attraction*

**Original:** A married man (Michael Douglas) has a one-night stand (Glenn Close) who comes back to haunt him when she devolves into the madwoman-turned-stalker in the face of unrequited love; she sets Douglas's car on fire, she boils his daughter's rabbit in a pot on his stove, she attacks Douglas' wife with a kitchen knife. They wrestle in the bathroom under a score of dramatic music and Close dies theatrically after being shot by the wife.

**Reimagined:** While his wife is out of town, Douglas spends a steamy weekend having athletic sex with his new colleague, played by Close. Douglas is smitten, but he doesn't need to hide it from his wife; and, in fact, instead of visiting her parents in the country, his wife is at a key party in New Jersey with her own lover (it is 1987, swinging is in vogue amongst wild suburbanites). Douglas's wife is pleased that this New Relationship Energy between her husband and his new lover has led to hotter sex between them and a sudden enthusiasm to whistle while doing the dishes. They invite Glenn Close for dinner. The women get along and lovingly make fun of Michael Douglas's snoring. They all eat bloodless vegetable stew for dinner, and the rabbit grows old and happy. The end.

**See also:** Unfaithful. Polyamory saves characters from a bloody end, once again.

# The Extramarital Affair:
## *Indecent Proposal*

**Original:** A billionaire (Robert Redford) offers one million dollars to a young married couple (Demi Moore and Woody Harrelson) for one night with the wife.

**Reimagined:** The chemistry between Redford and Moore is palpable and, though it's 1993, both men are comfortable with their masculinity and don't need a swinging dick contest to win Moore's attention; Moore is empowered to flirt with whomever she wants. There is a special spark between the men, too, but they convince themselves they are only interested in being naked with each other with Moore in between them. They play pool, laugh, and tap each other's backs in a manly way (the universal gesture for "no homo"). Instead of offering $1 million to spend a night with Moore and asking her husband if he can "borrow" her, Redford offers to lend them the money they need to save their house, and their attorney draws up a contract with reimbursement terms because they all have healthy boundaries and don't want money to taint their burgeoning polyamorous romance. The end.

**See also:** Forgetting Sarah Marshall. Nobody needs to forget Sarah Marshall for having sex with someone else, so no movie.

## The Lovers' Family Feud: *The Notebook*

**Original:** Seventeen-year-olds Rachel McAdams and Ryan Gosling fall madly in love while McAdams's family is visiting Gosling's small town in North Carolina for the summer. McAdams is from a rich family and is set to go off to college; Gosling is a lumber yard hunk. McAdams's mother interferes and keeps them apart after the summer is over. When the lovers meet again years later, McAdams is engaged to another man and is forced to make a choice.

**Reimagined:** Instead of calling her boyfriend trash and hiding the letters Gosling sends, McAdams's mother begs her to consider polyamory:

"But I want to be his and his only, Mama," McAdams cries.

"You're only seventeen," her mother replies sternly. "He's a nice boy, but he won't be able to fill all your needs. And trust me, you don't want the pressure of having to fulfill every single one of *his* needs for decades."

"You can't tell me what to do!" McAdams stammers.

"Oh yes I can," her mother screams back. "You *will* continue dating and you *will* have multiple partners who love you and support you and make you feel whole, you hear me?"

Two months later, McAdams falls in love with a rich young man during her first semester in New York. She asks her new boyfriend how he'd feel if she went to visit Gosling, her first love, for a few days. Instead of forcing her to choose, he tells her that while he feels jealous and possessive, he's going to work on managing his emotions.

McAdams's parents are thrilled to have two sons-in-law, one who travels and speaks foreign languages, and one who can restore an entire mansion with hand tools and passionately undress her in the rain. The end.

**See also:** Romeo + Juliet, Midsummer Night's Deam, Hamlet. Polyamory would likely ruin the entire Shakespearean cannon.

# ways of seeing my metamour

## Someone who loves my partner,
## and who my partner loves

I watched Don on stage, standing behind the podium in his brand-new navy suit, his beard freshly trimmed. I sat in the empty first row. Two-thirds of the seats were filled, but no one ever wants to sit in the first row. Don spoke with assurance and commanded the room, but I could see the sweat in his receding hairline, shiny under the fluorescent lighting of the carpeted hotel conference room. He pressed on his laptop to switch to a new graph on the screen.

I took a few photos to send to Bridget. She'd never seen him give a talk. I knew it would make her happy to see him in his element, but that she'd also recognize the peculiar hand gestures he does when he explains something complex that he's passionate about.

*I call this one "the claw,"* I texted with a picture of Don raising his right hand above the podium, fingers spread in a bear claw.

In the second picture, Don's thumb and index finger were pointed at the audience, to put emphasis on an argument he was making. *And this one, the pliers.*

I could have sent it to his mother and she would have laughed with maternal pride, or to one of my friends who would have found my captions clever, or to my own mother, who'd be happy to see me so obviously in love. But I knew Bridget would look at those pictures the way *I* would if I received them: Her brain would light up with warmth and excitement, she'd erupt in loving laughter, and she'd feel proud of both his career and their relationship. Sharing that feeling felt radical. I looked up at Don. He tapped a key on his laptop and the slide with his name and contact information appeared on the screen. The audience clapped and Don dabbed his forehead with the polka-dot pocket square I'd gifted him.

Before Don started dating Bridget, he had not yet experienced a stable second relationship. He'd dated around, but he had the most success at finding women interested in hookups, and by the time he met Bridget, he was hoping for something more substantial.

Don's first date with Bridget started with dinner in his neighborhood. I distracted myself with a Skype call with Lukas, then a run through the spring mud in Central Park, then a luscious vegan pizza. I was soaking in the hot bath, carefully holding an erotic novel by Anne Rice above the water, when my phone vibrated on the black and white tiled floor. *Leaving the restaurant, going to a bar nearby,* Don texted. I sighed, tossed the book on the floor, and looked at my shriveled fingertips. I turned the handle to add more hot water. Don was a great first date, particularly back when he still drank. He asked thoughtful questions better than anyone I'd dated, and he could drink a gallon of vodka without ever seeming buzzed. Even his bad dates lasted longer than my best ones. At 11 p.m., I was tossing and turning in his bed when Don's key finally clicked in the door. I heard him walk carefully down the hallway, stepping as lightly as he could without putting weight on the heel of his cowboy boots. "I'm still up," I yelled from the bedroom, and sat up against the headboard.

"Oh, hi sweetheart!" he yelled back. I heard the hallway closet open, the coat hangers clanking together, then the door latch closed. Don entered the bedroom and sat on the suede armchair in the corner in front of the bed.

"How was it?" I asked.

"Pretty good!" he said, putting one foot over his knee, pulling hard on one of his boots.

I walked to him and reached for his foot. With one hand behind the heel and the other on the toe tip, I squatted and pushed my weight to the back. The boot finally popped off.

"She's from the Midwest," he said "and I like her accent. She's the one who pitched polyamory to her partner, so I told her you were the one to get me into it. Oh and she's kinky."

The second boot popped off and I lost my balance, catching myself on the foot of the bed behind me.

Their relationship slowly deepened over the next three years. They were both in hierarchical non-monogamous structures— Bridget with Mike, Don with me—so their relationship inched along. Don respected her for her dedication to her business—and for the dominant energy she exuded. She liked that he was smart and empathic, and did research on the interaction of the brain and cardiovascular system; she had an anatomical drawing of a heart tattooed on her bicep.

While Don took charge of people at his research center and in most relationships, the two of them figured out that their dynamic worked best with Bridget in the lead. They each loved exploring a side of themselves they hadn't shown many other people, and they used their respective roles to express love and care for one another.

Don's submissive role with her was different from the natural dynamic we had in our relationship. With me, he set the tone and the pace, he was a caretaker, a guide, a mentor. The fact that Don was engaging this whole other dimension of himself, that had little to do with me, made me feel comfortable in a way I never expected.

So when I first realized that Bridget was in love with Don, and that he loved her back, it wasn't threatening to me. It felt natural, like it was on a totally separate frequency from the love I had for him.

## A projection of all my worst insecurities

I laid in bed with Don after his first date with Bridget, his bare feet interlaced with mine.

"Can you show me pictures of her?" I asked.

Don picked up his phone from his nightstand, pulled up her

OkCupid pictures, and passed it to me. Bridget's face was cropped out (as many non-monogamous folks' were in their profiles). In one picture, she lay on the floor in her underwear, her dancer body accentuated by the soft lighting. I worried that the newness of this incredibly sexy person, whose career was devoted to sculpting healthy bodies, would overpower the one-year-old attraction Don had for me.

"She looks beautiful," I said. I gave him the phone back and reached to my nightstand to turn my white noise machine on.

When I met Bridget for the first time, I was relieved: I didn't find her attractive. She was certainly beautiful, but I, myself, wasn't attracted to her. I knew *Don* found her attractive, but strangely, that wasn't what mattered.

Bridget had a grounded vibe. There was a power to her presence. She never spoke loudly, or too fast, like everyone complained I did all my life.

"Breathe between sentences and stop screaming, I'm right next to you," my mother told me as a kid.

"You walk too loudly," my roommates complained.

Don was the only person who'd never been too bothered by my volume. Every once in a while, he'd gently press his hand on my thigh while I spoke, a sign that I could lower my voice—which never made me feel bad.

Bridget took the time to think while she spoke. I could tell she didn't need to refrain from interrupting people. That is another thing I'd had to work on all my life. While I could be a very thoughtful listener in many contexts, sometimes the pace at which thoughts entered my brain made me worry I'd forget them if I didn't speak right away.

Bridget always had thoughtful outfits, flowing skirts and matching eyeshadow. The first time I was in her bathroom, my jaw dropped: handcrafted soap bars in shades of green, ochre, and cream on holders in the tub. On the windowsill, tall, skinny bottles of shampoo and conditioner for dyed hair. Several mascaras in metallic tubes in a small wire basket by the sink. On a shelf, face soap, scrub, and moisturizer in small glass containers. A whole eyeshadow briefcase sat on the floor between the toilet and the vanity. A *briefcase*. I didn't even own face wash. Or conditioner.

I was socialized as a girl growing up, but I was often called a tomboy. I'd learned to perform the role of *girl* the same way I learned how to play characters in my after-school theater program. Girlfriends in middle school taught me how to apply silver eyeliner like they did, and I gratefully accepted the clothes they no longer wanted, like Karine's suede platform shoes, or Maude's baby blue tube top.

Bridget loved organizing dinner parties, and knew how to cook colorful canapes and orchestrate evenings in a way that seemed effortless. I, on the other hand, was an anxious mess any time people came over, and always resorted to buying premade food (I never could talk and cook at the same time, and every recipe took me triple the promised preparation time). My mother was the same. We often laughed about the time she messed up a Jell-O recipe, and the time I ruined rice (the inability to measure quantities and attentively read a recipe was apparently genetic). That felt like another part of femininity that I failed at.

Comparing oneself with a metamour is normal at first. When a partner is infatuated with someone else, social scripts prescribe jealousy and envy as the logical response. I had a lot to unlearn.

## Subordinate in my love hierarchy

I stood on the 1 train, holding a wet umbrella in one hand, and the handrail above my head with the other. Don stood next to me as I faced forward on the train to avoid motion sickness.

"Do you know what you're getting Bridget for her birthday?" I asked.

"Probably tickets to some dance show," he said, "and we'll do dinner beforehand."

"Didn't you do that last Christmas?" I asked more loudly, to cover the noise of a baby crying and someone listening to a video without headphones.

"Probably," Don replied.

Don has a terrible memory. What he doesn't remember genuinely has nothing to do with how much he cares.

He and I didn't make big deals out of our birthdays, but for Bridget, October was her birthday *month*, and it was important to celebrate it. I let the umbrella fall on the train floor in between my khaki rain boots and pulled my phone out of my pocket to look at our shared calendar.

"How would you feel about offering her a weekend away with you?" I asked.

"Really?" he said.

"Yeah," I replied. "I think it would be nice for you two to experience that, and I think we're ready. I trust both of you."

"That's very thoughtful of you, sweetheart," Don said. "I'll ask her." He leaned in towards my lips and the train braked suddenly, making our kiss wobbly.

I sat on Bridget's vintage green loveseat, while she slid open the sepia globe of her antique bar cart, and pulled out a whiskey bottle. It was the week after she and Don returned from Hudson.

"I have to admit," she said while pouring whiskey into her glass, "that going on that trip with Don made me feel uncomfortable at first."

"How?" I asked.

She sat down on an armchair in front of me. "Out of town trips feel like they should be reserved for primary partners. It always felt normal to take them with Mike, but it was the first time I had one with someone else. And I know it's just social conditioning, but that lizard brain is powerful."

She tapped the base of her skull right above her neck for emphasis. Bridget often talked about needing to deprogram her "lizard brain," which usually meant discarding something the patriarchy had engrained: the desire to wear a white dress and a ring, and to live within the comfortable framework of a pair that takes priority over everyone else in life. I'd struggled with it too, but Bridget's shackles were tighter.

"Did you enjoy it?" I asked.

"I did," she said, smiling. "It was really nice to spend uninterrupted time together for two days. I don't think we had ever done two sleepovers in a row before." The kettle whistled, and Bridget continued talking while walking to the adjacent kitchen. "And taking the train together was fun, though I would have loved to drive. There are a lot of little things I still haven't experienced with Don even though we've been together for quite a while. Like I don't even know what he's like in a car."

She handed me a handmade brown mug of fragrant ginger tea.

"Nervous and annoying," I replied laughing into my mug before taking a slow sip. I set it on a cork coaster. "He'll always avoid driving if he can."

I felt proud of myself for having opened the door for them to share this experience together. But it wasn't a selfless offer. Even though I didn't have a partner other than Don at that time, I knew that I had wanted to take trips with my ex, and that I would want to again with someone one day. I liked to believe that Bridget was slowly becoming a peer instead of a subordinate in the relationship hierarchy, but *I* was the one who suggested the trip. I controlled the giving of this "gift," which made it more like a favor and not a right.

Unlike with my ex, that didn't seem like an issue for Bridget: She felt comfortable in a tight, hierarchical polyamorous relationship. She probably wanted to wield the same power with Mike, or whomever she ended up with for the long haul.

Bridget bent down from her seat to reach her animal spirit tarot deck. She lifted the white box, illustrated with one yellow eye wrapped with reptilian scales.

"Want me to pull a card for you?"

## A friend-sibling-companion who's always just out of reach

Before Bridget, I never felt the power of a metamour bond. Don had a few partners that were around for strings of weeks at a time, but I never clicked with them. One had a high-pitched, nasal voice that scratched my insides, another answered most of my questions with single words. But Bridget was present in conversations, and I liked that she initiated her journey into polyamory on her own and looked for partners interested in joining her, like me. "Monogamy was a coat that never fit quite right," she told me over tea in a bright cafe with floor-to-ceiling windows and funky patterned curtains. She raised her hands by her head and wiggled as if her movements were constricted by an imaginary coat over her white tank top. I felt seen. She was a kindred spirit.

Bridget crouched in a deep yogi squat in my backyard, barefoot, the soles of her feet resting on the ground. She pulled a coleus plant out of a black plastic pot. I liked the bright pink color in the middle of the deep green leaves.

"So before you transplant," she said, "you want to loosen the roots, like this." She gently spread the roots apart and soil crumbed down at her feet. I nodded, on my hands and knees next to the empty garden bed, and continued digging a hole with a trowel.

"I can't believe you were able to snatch this apartment before it went on the market," Bridget said and dipped the plant in a mix of water and fish emulsion. The sun was blazing for early June. Sweat coated Bridget's muscular shoulder blades, exposed by her racerback yellow tank top. I was never able to keep houseplants alive, but, invigorated by the extreme luxury of a small private backyard that came with my ground floor studio, I asked Bridget to teach me how to garden.

"You know," I said, wiping my hands on my white tank top, "I saw that the unit across the hall was just put on the market. Wouldn't it be great if we lived in the same building?"

"Oh my god, Don would either love it or hate it," Bridget replied, laughing.

"I'm serious though," I said, handing her her green water bottle. "I know you won't leave your rent-controlled apartment, but figuring out how to get the whole polycule in one building would make me so happy."

"I know, that's the dream," she said.

Bridget helping me with my garden made me feel like I was on the path to building a true home in New York for the first time.

A few years later, I'd quit my tech job to become a farmer.

"Hey friend," Bridget started to say every time she greeted me. Even though she said *friend*, the way she said it sounded deeper, more familial. When I started performing a storytelling show about my early polyamorous explorations, she saw it *five* times. I always found her in the audience, sitting upright, her bright gray eyes watching me with utmost attention. Her deep laughs sent small bursts of energy up my spine.

Still, the vulnerable moments we shared were rare. There was a certain distance to Bridget, and I found it difficult to completely let my walls down with her. Maybe it was because I was still working on deprogramming my own lizard brain. Or maybe it was that I was the one reaching out to her most of the time. Sometimes it would take a few days before she'd answer a text. She always showed up when it mattered, but I couldn't help but feel like she was a greater priority for me than I was for her.

After she transitioned to a secondary partnership with Mike, this distance grew. Bridget would say her next availability to hangout wasn't for two weeks, then she'd tell me about last minute dates she scheduled. I didn't blame her: I essentially had what she was looking for, and I understood the deep yearning for an anchor partner. But I was longing for a long-term relationship with her, too. An intimate metamour bond, I'd discovered, was one of the best benefits of polyamory, and I wanted more.

## Someone who hurts my partner

I'd never seen Don in pain before. He took most things in stride. He tried to model emotion regulation for me. "Good times are always followed by bad times, then good times again," he'd tell me when I was in one of my cyclical lows. He'd seen me devastated when Lukas had broken up with me two years prior. He reminded me that breakups often have little to do with the worth the dumper sees in the dumpee, and are, instead, about the circumstances of the dumper's life and how they complement ours or not. Still, when Bridget left him, he was sad.

When Don struggled, he tended to focus on work or statistical analyses for fantasy football, rather than talk about his suffering. When I'd press him on his emotions, he would say seemingly healthy, insightful things that suggested he was much further down the path of processing than I thought he actually was. Maybe it showed his wisdom, or maybe it was just the words that came reflexively after years of psychology training. But it was clear that the breakup affected him.

On a Sunday, he still laid in bed at noon, holding his phone sideways against his bare stomach. A space documentary narrated by a deep British voice played. Don loved his large flat screen TV, but it was the third Sunday in a row that he didn't make it to the living room. I slid in bed next to him, and pressed into his side. I brushed my lips on his cheek, and gave him a series of short kisses. He gave me *fish kisses* back—that's what we called those—but they were slower than usual.

A year before, Bridget had gone through a relationship transition with her primary partner, Mike. Bridget wanted to adopt kids and cohabitate full time with someone. Mike didn't want to co-parent and liked his own space. They spent five days a week together, but having separate places was important to him.

In a monogamous context, these would have been grounds for dissolving the partnership. But we'd all started looking at relationships from a more flexible perspective, and knew that breakups were not always necessary. A relationship could transition to something different to meet the evolving needs of the partners involved. We had friends who'd done it. So, Bridget and Mike decided to move to a secondary relationship model, and she started looking for her anchor partner, with whom she'd be able to share the things she wanted in her future. At that point, Bridget saw both Don and Mike once a week.

Then, Bridget began a new relationship with someone who took her on trips to places with beaches, and she liked how it felt to be with someone who signaled they might commit to her in the way she had always wanted Mike to. I loved that for her, because she would finally get to build the type of life she needed.

When Bridget broke up with Don to focus on building a foundation with her new partner, with plans to reopen their relationship in the future, it took me by surprise. Don and I had only met Bridget's partner once, when we crossed paths at a show and didn't have the chance to exchange much more than introductions. I was concerned Bridget was settling for someone who didn't accept *all* of her. She'd been so adamant that monogamy wasn't for her, and that building a kind of family with her partners and metamours was crucial. It was possible she'd truly changed her mind about the type of non-monogamy she wanted, but I had no way of knowing if she was actually happy since she was growing more distant, and I'd never seen her with her new partner. If we had met a few times before their relationship took this same turn, I wouldn't have been as resentful. But Bridget had broken up with *Don*, not me, so I suppressed my own grief.

## An ex who isn't quite an ex

Don re-entered the hospital room in a blue gown, his clothes stuffed in a clear plastic bag.

"You didn't even tie your gown in the back!" I said, forcing myself to chuckle.

"Oh they see hairy butts all day long," he replied. "I wouldn't worry about that. Plus, most of their patients aren't as sexy as me..."

Still standing in the doorway, he pulled his gown up and lifted his thigh, toes seductively pointed on the floor. I rose up from the chair set next to the bed, smiled and took a picture of his pose. I knew he was trying to set a mood that meant *this wasn't a big deal.* In the five years we'd been together, I'd pictured him dying or falling seriously ill hundreds, maybe thousands, of times. I'd always imagined it would be around his 51st birthday, the age my father was when he had his stroke. Since then, I've had intrusive thoughts about all my loved ones suddenly dying or getting sick. Every time I'd voice my fears, Don patiently held me and said he'd live healthily for a very, very long time. But there he was, at forty, about to undergo heart surgery.

After he collapsed in the kitchen, we discovered he had a genetic arrhythmia.

I sat on the blue vinyl chair in Don's office, grateful that his research center was in the hospital and that I had a quiet place to cry. I had a pile of memoirs and hours of crime podcasts saved on my phone. *The procedure can take anywhere between three and ten hours,* a nurse had told us, shaking her head and raising her palms. I looked at the books at my feet and didn't pick any up. I turned the fluorescent light on, and turned it off. I walked to the wall behind his desk and looked at the row of diplomas. He had finally gotten them framed, ten years after his last graduation. I sat on the floor, leaning on his desk.

Bridget had broken up with Don the year before. He was over her, but I still missed her. We texted here and there, but it seemed inappropriate to call her now. Don had started dating someone new, Aly, but she and I weren't close yet.

The success rate of Don's procedure was extremely high, so my rational brain trusted everything would be fine, and that his arrhythmia would be gone afterwards. But I also imagined being in a waiting room ten, twenty years down the road, a doctor telling me they couldn't save him. That future grief already cinched my insides. I opened my text thread with Bridget and scrolled up, and up, and up. I turned the phone screen off.

# polyamory as seen in eleven places

## Customs

"How do you all know each other?" the Border Patrol Agent asks, his eyes narrowed into me. His jaw is pulled forward, accentuating his red beard. I'm at the wheel, Don is reclined in the passenger seat, and Kate is buckled in the back. Don and I drove up to Montreal to visit my family and are bringing her back to New York with us. I notice that I'm tapping my left foot and stop myself. Agents are trained to pick up on signs of anxiety, I'm sure. Even though I'm a model border crosser, I get the leg bounce every time. Years ago, when I was still on a student visa, I remembered a clementine I'd left in my backpack as I approached the checkpoint. My chest pounded while I stretched my hand to the passenger side to rummage through the bag. When I found it, I fired the clementine out the passenger window toward a billboard that read, "Hors Taxes / Duty Free." Still, my left knee jittered for miles.

I consider potential responses to the agent's question: *We know each other...intimately?* I want to say. But I tell him my husband and I are bringing back my high school friend with us, and she'll fly back to Québec in a week. It isn't a lie, though it feels like one.

## U.S. Citizenship and Immigration Services Office

"Do you plan to practice polygamy in the United States?" the officer asks mechanically. His pen is upright, prepared to check the box on his form. A plexiglass partition separates my chair from the imposing wooden desk behind which the officer sits. He is surprisingly friendly, but no matter how wide his smile is or how many poutine anecdotes he tells, the pressure in my ribcage won't ease.

"No," I reply. The government's definition of polygamy is "the custom of having more than one spouse at the same time." They ask this to everyone passing the U.S. citizenship exam, as polygamy is illegal in the United States. I researched the legality of my polyamory thoroughly during many late-night Googling sessions. *You cannot be considered a practicing polygamist unless you belong to a culture or religion that recognizes the custom of polygamy,* I read. Still, I worried that my polyamory could raise a red flag in my immigration process "Don't lie if they ask directly," my attorney had said, "but definitely don't volunteer the information." At the end of the interview, the officer declares he'll recommend my application be approved, and closes his folder. When I exit the building through the too-slow revolving doors and see Don waving at me, I shed tears of relief.

## Work

"I'm taken more seriously at work now that I have a wedding ring on," Don says, comfortably seated in his recliner, tearing the tin-foil around his burrito. I'm on the carpet, elbows perched on the coffee table, biting into mine. He says it with detachment, as a simple fact, but I feel the same way and it angers me. I wear my ring at the nonprofit where I work and when I go through customs, but otherwise I don't.

"I bet if people found out the nature of our relationship," I tell him, "they wouldn't see it the same way." I open a small plastic container and pour hot sauce on my burrito. You go up in the world when you get married. You go down when people find out it's polyamorous.

## Driveway

I exit the side door of my little house and follow my girlfriend down the poorly-shoveled path to her car. Snowflakes land in her raven curls, contained by her tan felt beret. I love her in that beret.

"Hi Kristi," she says to my neighbor. "It's me, Cara!" My next-door neighbor is standing near the curb between our driveways, with two other women who live on our street. Their faces are hard to see in the moonless night.

"Cara?" Kristi says, fog coming out of her mouth. "I didn't know you two knew each other!"

I've lived in the Hudson Valley for almost a year and moved into the house for the winter a few weeks prior. It's a small community; everyone is connected to each other in one way or another. My neighbors have already met Don, who comes up from New York City to spend half his time with me.

"Yeah," I say to my neighbor Kristi. "She's my girlfriend."

"How long have you been friends?" Kristi asks.

"We mean we're in a *relationship*," Cara says, enunciating slowly and waving her index finger between us.

"Oh, that's...great," Kristi says slowly, taking a mittened hand out of her pocket and scratching her nose. She glances at her boots, then falls silent.

## Home

My landlord calls to ask something about the heating and mentions he'll be in town for the weekend. My stomach buzzes with apprehension. I rise from my desk and slowly walk around the coffee table, my soles pressing in the teal rug.

"Just so you know," I try to say matter-of-factly, "I'll be away for the weekend and Don will be in the house with his girlfriend."

Through my living room window, I can see the parked camper he stays in.

Seconds pass.

"I thought you and Don were married," he says.

"We are," I reply. I don't know which is stronger: my sense of shame, or my irritation.

"I thought I was renting to a *couple*," he says.

"We *are* a couple," I insist. I sit on the coffee table. "We're polyamorous, meaning we also have other relationships."

"I don't want to seem backwards," he says. "It's just that even if I rent it out, it's my house, and I didn't know there'd be a bunch of people in and out."

I apologize for the confusion and assure him that we take good care of the house. But what I want to say is: We're not up all night hosting orgies. I've lost more sleep trying to manage our shared Google calendars than I have fucking other people.

## Gynecologist

I pull the pen from the clipboard that the too-joyous Ob/Gyn receptionist handed me.

*Do you have a partner?*

I check "yes" and look up at the blue shapes in the abstract painting on the wall to my right. I look down at the form and tap my pen on the side of the clipboard. I carefully add parentheses around the "a" and add "(s)" to "partner," so that it reads *Do you have (a) partner(s)?* I also add "(s)" to the "gender" line below, and write *cis woman, cis man.*

I glance at the receptionist, wondering what reaction he'll have when he reads my form. I flip the page and sigh when I see the emergency contact field has room for only one person. I add Aly's name under Don's, in letters small enough to fit above the next form item. Under *relationship*, I write *family* because the line isn't long enough to explain polyamory.

## Walgreens

I open and close cards in the anniversary section. I pull one with a dark sky and a shooting star with big bold letters that say *You complete my universe.* I put it back and squeeze myself against the rack to let a shopper in polka dot shorts and heart-shaped yellow sunglasses pass me. I pull another card that unfolds in a large accordion and tells *The Story of Us: A Modern Fairy Tale.* I don't need to read the whole thing to know how it ends. I'm looking for a card that doesn't emphasize the one and *only.* I continue pulling cards and slipping them back in the rack, my movements getting faster and jerkier. I want to take out a sharpie and make edits.

*To my better half* THIRD (JUST JOKING. I'M WHOLE EVEN WITHOUT YOU, BUT YOU DO MAKE MY LIFE BETTER)

*You are my storybook love, the woman of my dreams.* WE'LL HAVE TO HUMANS WRITE OUR OWN ONE OF STORYBOOK

JUST
*I can't imagine sharing life's journey with anyone but you.*

ONE OF

*You're the best things that ever happened to me.*

ALONG WITH MY OTHER PARTNER, ALL
MY CLOSE FRIENDS, ANTIDEPRESSANTS,
AND OLIVES.

*For the woman I love...I love you more than barbecue. I love you
more than beer. I love you more than power tools -and- classic
episodes of manly action tv shows where lots of stuff explodes! I
love you more than nacho chips and more than basketball.*

FUCK THIS GENDER-NORMATIVE BULLSHIT

I walk down the aisle, to the *Without Text* section. I pull one
with a watercolor of two parrots embracing and walk to the ca-
shier.

## My Head

I lean against the clawfoot tub propped on a pile of palettes, and
reach in with both hands to scoop a large amount of soil mix and
drop it on a seed tray. The sound of the April rain resonates across
the greenhouse. I always find the smell of the wood burning stove
and wet soil calming. It's just me and Kai working at the farm
today; it's their first day. They dump a wheelbarrow load of wood
chips, then spread them with a rake to cover the muddy walkway
between the tables. We've been chatting to get to know each
other.

"I'm polyamorous," I tell them, scraping my hand across the

tray to even out the soil in each square cell. "Meaning I have multiple romantic partners." I'm proud of myself for putting it out there right away, without tiptoeing around it. I've been working on this for a while.

"Yeah, I know polyamory" they reply, "I'm also polyamorous. Solo-poly."

Oh. My delight of having found a potential non-monogamous friend is tempered by my embarrassment. Why did I assume they were monogamous?

## Restaurant

My two dates and I sit at a round table in the corner of a dark tapas place in Hell's Kitchen. Acoustic Spanish guitar plays on the speakers.

"Well done finding this place," Peter says to me.

"Yeah, this looks great," Trish adds, and leans in to peck my lips.

I unwrap my silverware and lay the tan cloth on my lap.

"Actually," I say, and playfully gesture for them to lean in closer with my index fixer. "I looked at inside photos on Yelp and then called to specifically reserve a round table."

"Ah! *Your best triad table, please!*" Peter says and we all chuckle.

This is our third date. On our second, we played rock paper scissors to decide which one of us would have to sit in front of an empty chair at the rectangular table for four.

I look down at my menu, printed on a delicate sheet strapped to a small wooden board with rubber bands. They have two sections: à la carte, and a set menu for two.

## Wedding

I sit at my desk in my lime sweatpants, and pull my laptop open and click on a new email from a friend.

*Dear Alex & Guest,*

*We're making it official on May 1st and you're invited! You are welcome to bring a plus one.*

I feel a jolt of joy. A few years back, I encouraged Nicole to pursue her interest in our mutual friend, and they were now getting married! I liked to think I played a part in that. I look out the window in front of my desk. The sun is rising in the valley, and the fog hangs low on the snow covered mountains. I wonder if I want to bring Don or Aly to that wedding. It's in Spain, and I can't imagine going on a big trip without Aly. Maybe we can make it a family trip with the three of us, but only two of us go to the actual wedding? Don does know the bride and groom already, so maybe it would make the most sense to bring him. But how would that make Aly feel?

## Housewarming

"Doesn't one of you feel like a third wheel?" a new acquaintance asks me after I explain that I'm in a triad.

I pull the lemon slice off my glass rim and pop it in my seltzer. I smile playfully. "What's wrong with a tricycle?" I ask.

# triad / triptych

## I. Kate

Don exchanged a look with my childhood friend, and I saw it:
Even though he had only known her for two hours, he could love
her. Kate sat on our low sectional with her legs folded under her,
knees pointed toward Don. She ran her hand through her long
brown hair and brushed it over her shoulder, like she often did,
exposing her delicate neck. She belonged on our couch. Though
Don and I had been polyamorous for our entire year-and-a-half
relationship, we'd never dated someone together, never mind
someone I had been close with since we were thirteen. At this
unexpected prospect, I was both threatened and turned on.

Kate and I went to middle school together. She was visiting
me for the first time since I'd moved to New York City for grad
school four years earlier, when I was newly single. She knew I
ditched monogamy as soon as I crossed the border, so in the
weeks leading up to her visit, Kate joked that she was coming for

her "polyamorous internship." She'd just broken up with someone, and having cheated on almost everyone she'd ever dated,
she was intrigued by ethical non-monogamy.

Don's legs were stretched out on the chaise of our sectional
while Kate sat on the middle cushion, close to him. She listened to
Don, nodding along, as her perfectly ironed curls bobbed up and
down. Her brown eyebrows furrowed with attention, and her
grayish blue eyes were particularly dazzling tonight. Don was reclined comfortably, one arm on the backrest behind Kate, silver
hair poked out of his black v-neck. Through the windows behind
them, the distant lights from New Jersey skyscrapers across the
Hudson River were barely visible, and the streets were quiet except
for the occasional hoots of Columbia students heading for the bars
on Amsterdam. I sat on our shag rug, facing them, tucked in the
corner the couch. I liked seeing them from that vantage point;
both participant and observer. Kate sometimes touched my shoulder and Don's forearm to punctuate her comments. Don gently
rubbed my neck with one hand, and briefly touched Kate's knee a
few times.

I'd never experienced attraction as overwhelming as this—it
was pulling the three of us together. Our three-way desire heightened each individual relationship: the deep intimacy between her
and me, the infatuation at first sight between her and him, and
the unconditional love between him and me. My insides were
boiling with a tangled mess of lust, fear, thrill, and loaded questions that threatened to upend every assumption I had previously
held about my future.

Kate had prepared a list of questions for me and Don. Of
course she'd prepared a list. This was one of the many reasons I
adored Kate.

"Do you consult the other before you have sex or date someone?" Kate asked, reading from her phone.

"It depends on the situation," I said, looking up at Kate. "In most cases we meet people online so we always know when we go on dates and that it's a possibility sex will happen. Say I met someone while at a party at a friend's house, and ended up making out or something, then I wouldn't need to stop it and call Don. But if it was going towards sex, I'd probably send a quick text."

Don laid his hand on my shoulder. "Some people give each other veto power," he said, "and I tried that early on when Alex met Lukas, but we learned quick enough that it just doesn't work and isn't really ethical."

"C'est quoi *vitto*?" Kate asked me.

"Comme un droit de véto."

"Aaah!" she exclaimed, leaning her head back. "*Veto*. Oui ok."

"You know, Kate," Don said, putting his wine glass on the windowsill next to the couch. "Your Québécois accent reminds me of what Alex's sounded like when we met. It was adorable. Still is, it just was extra adorable."

We opened a second bottle of wine, then a digestif Kate had brought.

"I was never a great girlfriend," she said, playing with her hair. "I find that I am better at completing a couple."

I heard the obvious unasked question. I knew I was the one in charge of acknowledging it. But my blood rushed up and left my body, and I turned to stone. Don had been stirring our conversation with open-ended questions, as he automatically did as a trained therapist, but this time he stayed silent, and looked at me.

If I acknowledged the sexual tension in the room, I feared it would have implications for the rest of my life.

I switched to French, unconsciously creating distance between them to cool down the room. "I remember you telling me this after spending your holidays in France with your friend and her partner. What were their names again?" I asked Kate.

At the end of the night, I tucked Kate in on the couch. I kneeled on the rug next to her, lingering before I joined Don in the bedroom. My anxious uncertainty had lit a spotlight on my every movement, and caused sweat to coat my palms. It felt wrong to let her sleep alone in the living room. "Bonne nuit," she said. The charcoal wool blanket was tucked under her armpits, and her face cream made her skin glisten in the dimmed light. I bent down and she raised her chin to give me the customary cheek kisses. Our cheeks touched, and I remembered what her lips tasted like.

Kate was the first girl I ever kissed. During our first kiss, our teeth knocked together. I have thin lips and big teeth, and it wasn't easy to maneuver as a fourteen-year-old inexperienced kisser. But we'd applied ourselves, and with practice, we refined our technique. Again, and again. Over the years, we slept together twice, but it had always been initiated on a dance floor after one too many drinks, and ended in guilt; we had both been in monogamous relationships. This time, I was clear headed. I could cup her face in my hands and kiss her, guilt-free. I mumbled, "Bonne nuit," and fled to the bedroom.

All my non-monogamous relationships had been parallel; my partners sporadically hung out with each other like in-laws. Part of my initial draw to polyamory was my desire to remain an *individual*; to embody different parts of myself that came out through the distinct types of intimacy I had with different people. Could I be both the person Kate knew from back home *and* the person I was with Don? Could I share her with him, and him with her?

In bed, in the faint red light of our night lamp, I told Don I regretted not kissing her. "I never saw you look at Bridget the way you looked at her tonight," I said. I put my cheek on his shoulder, and he gently squeezed the back of my neck.

"I think it's easier for me to really go there when you're also a part of it," he said. "I like Bridget and I know I'm allowed to fall for her, but there is still some preprogrammed something that tells me it's wrong."

I lifted my head up to look at him. His cheeks were freshly shaven but he'd missed a hair high on his cheekbone. I brushed my finger on it. "I think I'd like to try to see what happens if we open ourselves to her," I said.

The next evening, I came home after a late workday. I hated my tech job, and I found my carpeted office depressing. Would I have stayed in the U.S. after I graduated if I hadn't met Don? With its proud ignorance of the rest of the world and ridiculous healthcare system? Maybe not.

The shotgun kitchen was right in front of the apartment entrance. I opened the door to Kate, in a black tunic dress, spreading crackers on a plate and singing vocal riffs along a jazzy song. *Allô!* she said, and wiped her fingers on a towel. I smiled wide and hung my coat on a hook inside the closet door. Kate was preparing an *apéro*: there was red wine, cheese, *saucisson*, and a dubious "baguette" from the bakery on Broadway.

I closed the closet and took three steps to the kitchen entrance. I gave Kate a kiss on each cheek, and she asked how my day was.

"Une grosse journée de merde," I answered. It was satisfying to feel my Rs in the back of my throat when I spoke.

Kate was a *sommelière* and a fine dining consultant. She always managed to present food artfully, even on my chipped Ikea plates.

I crossed the entryway and turned left to walk into the living room. Don sat on the couch reading the news on his phone, his daily after-work routine. He stood up and walked around the yellow coffee table to kiss me hello, then he pulled me in and hugged me tightly. I rested my head on his shoulder for a moment, my forehead nested behind his jaw, his beard tickling my nose. "Welcome home," he said. He always said that, but *home* had never felt this complete.


We spent the evening listening to music and laughing. I sat so close to Kate on the couch that our knees touched, hers covered in sheer black tights, mine in jeans. When she turned her head away to look at Don, I smelled the pear blossom in her shampoo, her signature scent.

She turned to me, and brought her face ever so slightly closer to mine. An invitation. I'd thought about this moment all day. I leaned forward and I plunged.

When I'd navigated threesomes before, it had been hard to give myself in with abandonment. I was aware of every hand, every body placement. I worried about everyone feeling equally satisfied, tracking who received attention and how. This time, I trusted and loved them both. I didn't need to perform for anyone. It was beautiful to witness Kate and Don consummate their new infatuation. My role as the igniter felt special. I experienced no jealousy—on the contrary; seeing them exchange looks of passion and hearing their accelerated breaths interspersed with kisses was endearing and incredibly arousing.

The next morning, Kate brought us coffee in bed. The eastern sun flooded the room, and the radiator emitted loud streaming sounds. Kate had fished our dusty Italian espresso maker out of the cupboard, and even warmed up some milk. She sat at the foot of the bed, facing us, every single hair tucked perfectly into her ponytail. I never ceased to be amazed by—and envious of—how perfect she looked in the morning. In that moment, I wished I could savor her romantic attention all on my own, without Don. My third sip left me unsettled: Usually *I* made coffee for Don, and mine didn't taste nearly this good.

Five months later, Kate came to New York again. We scheduled her visit so she'd be able to attend the first reading of my solo storytelling show.

I'd started to go to open mics, but five-minute slots were too short for the deeper stories about my journey towards non-monogamy that I wanted to tell.

"Why don't you write a whole show?" Don asked, after I practiced an act in our living room, standing in my snowflake pajamas pants between the TV and the coffee table. I laughed.

"Who is going to come see this?" I said, and sat on the rug cross-legged.

"Just write it," he said, and put his feet on the coffee table.

Don always convinced me I could do anything.

Four months later, I invited ten friends over to hear my script and give feedback. Kate was ecstatic to be a part of it. As teenagers, we had sleepovers in a tent on her patio and wrote absurdist plays and oddly macabre songs. We performed sketch comedy for our presentations in French literature class.

Kate helped me rehearse, and suggested blocking for specific moments, to make something funnier or more poignant. I'd missed collaborating on artistic projects with her.

Kate and Don took care of the *hors-d'oeuvres* and wine selection for the event. Hosting and preparing food for guests always made me anxious. While Kate and Don moved the couch, unfolded chairs, and set up a food area, I was able to focus on rehearsing, and containing my stage fright.

Every time I glanced up during my reading, Kate's face was focused, reacting to my every word, her red lips parted. She nodded, frowned at the vulnerable moments, and laughed loudly at the self-deprecating ones. Her singular laugh—a crescendo I'd heard resonate in our high school classrooms—always made me smile.

Don was sitting next to Kate. His hand was on hers. As lucky as I felt to have both of their love and support as I was baring myself in this show, and as beautiful as they were—holding hands, loving me, sharing affection with one another—I also felt a tinge of resentment. We hadn't talked about displays of affection yet. They knew how vulnerable I already felt, sharing my writing and my personal stories for the first time. Couldn't they have predicted that it would be overwhelming for me to read my lines while learning to see my childhood friend and lover and my husband love on each other?

After four nights together, I began to feel claustrophobic. I was exhausted. I felt like there was nowhere to escape to. The three of us in a one-bedroom apartment. Everywhere I looked I saw Don's hand on her neck, her hand on his knee, the infatuated looks they exchanged. Kate's cuddles no longer felt sweet, they felt suffocating. Don's kisses reminded me that I was hiding my feelings from him, which I usually never did. I was so overwhelmed I couldn't express any of my desires. I couldn't ask for space, I couldn't ask them to slow down. I was drowning in the force of our three-way romance.

We ate sundried tomato paninis for lunch Sunday afternoon around the coffee table in the living room. Kate was scheduled to fly back to Montreal later that evening, at the end of her four-day trip.

"Ah merde," Kate said with her mouth full, looking at her phone. "Air Canada texted that my flight was canceled."

"*Canceled,* or delayed?" I asked, looking at Kate in front of me on the other side of the table. I felt my face warming.

"Canceled," Kate said. They are putting me on another flight tomorrow night.

This felt like a punch in my throat. My heart pumped and the edges of my vision blurred. I needed out of the vortex.

"I'm sorry..." Kate said. "Maybe I can look at the bus schedule." Kate looked at me and I avoided her gaze by focusing on my plate.

"The bus is miserable," Don said. "Stay until tomorrow, it's no problem."


I went to bed early, but insisted Don and Kate stay up and spend time together. I didn't have the right to declare our romantic weekend done because I was freaking out.

In bed, I couldn't sleep. I wept, I screamed into my pillow. I was so bitter that neither of them were checking on me. I hadn't expressed any of my struggles and had told them not to worry about me, but they should have *known*.

It dawned on me that maybe I couldn't do polyamory. This was not what polyamory looked like, my best friend and my husband probably having steamy sex on the couch while I snotted all over my sheets in the bedroom. I had just written a whole show celebrating my non-monogamy, preaching it made me happy.

In the week after Kate left, I slowly came back to myself. I should have known to plan breathing room and alone time, and not spend four days straight with two of the most intense people I know and love in a small apartment. Don asked me if I wanted to take a step back and focus on a platonic friendship with Kate. I didn't, or I wasn't sure if I did. The long-distance nature of our relationship naturally kept the pace slow. I just needed more breaks and time to myself during Kate's next visit.

Don and I ended up visiting Kate a couple of times, and some of our dynamic felt good and exciting, but something never felt quite right. When Kate met someone new who wasn't open to non-monogamy, we transitioned back to a platonic relationship. Kate remained a part of our life, as "just a friend," but with a lingering special closeness. I was relieved. Maybe the combination of the three of us at this time in our lives wasn't the right thing. Or maybe triads were not for me?

## II. Sophia

"Would you two be open to dating me together?" Sophia asked Don and me, unprompted. "I'm feeling a lot of chemistry."

Don sat in our new mid-century recliner, angled towards the couch. He wore a blue and gray plaid flannel shirt and both his arms laid on the armrests, widening his posture. I found him magnificent. Sophia and I sat on the sectional, with her closest to Don. She wore bright harem pants and sparkly sneakers with a thick sole that she kicked off before folding her legs under her. She smiled, flipping her head back and forth between Don and me.

It was a warm March day in the city; the leaves of Red Maple trees had just started poking out. I found Sophia's boldness attractive. I felt my heart rate double and my breathing quicken. Hiding my reaction only made it worse. I looked at Don and waited for him to answer, happy to lean on him.

I'd met Sophia on OkCupid two weeks before. On our first date—sitting at a bustling Mexican brunch spot in our neighborhood—she spoke passionately about teaching middle school, gently waving her hands when she spoke, and I was seduced. She wore a white and blue linen top with large buttons, and her thick dark hair fell over her shoulders, strikes of dyed burgundy accentuating her natural waves. I loved her voice. She spoke with melody, and her face lit up in a way that further animated her rapid shifts from a hushed near-whisper that pulled me in, to high pitched squeals of wonder and delight. I imagined her young students entranced by her lectures. She had a beautiful wide nose with a small stud piercing, and her nostrils stretched when she smiled.

On our second date, Sophia and I went to see a play directed by her partner's partner. On our third date, she invited me as a guest to her gym. After our yoga class, we changed out of our clothes by the wood paneled lockers. Electro-classical music played over the speakers, complemented by hair dryer background sounds. Standing next to me, she slid her dampened clothes off, exposing her pear hips and clementine breasts. The air was humid and smelled of eucalyptus. A hunger flooded my whole body and without thinking, I took her hand, picked up two white towels from a folded pile, and led her to the shower. Her eyes widened with surprise and anticipation, and she followed me with a grin on her face. She looked around as we passed the row of bowl sinks, wondering if someone would stop us. No one did.

We stepped into the shower stall and I closed the frosted glass door behind us. We shared our first kiss under the water and washed one another gently, the soap foam falling down at our feet on the textured eggshell tiles. Afterwards, she asked if she could meet Don.

The two of us walked into Don's and my apartment, buzzing from each other's touch.

Sophia waited for our answer to her fearless question.

"I won't speak for Alex," Don said, "but we had a brief long-distance triad dynamic with a close friend of theirs, who they'd been intimate with in the past, and I think both of us enjoyed that very much. But I also know that Alex is excited about you, and they've been looking forward to dating a woman on their own."

He was right. I was frustrated that, in less than an hour, Don had already charmed Sophia—*my* date. I had experienced few opportunities to embody my queerness. It was hard enough to meet a queer woman who was interested in me—a pansexual who dated cisgender heterosexual men—never mind finding one who was open to polyamory *and* with whom I had chemistry. Sophia was a *perle rare*. Even if Don indicated he would step aside, it didn't feel good to have to ask him to *let me* have her. Plus, I feared that Sophia would see me as less desirable alone—not in a package with Don. At the same time, with Don joining us, I felt my potential relationship with her become exponentially more enticing.

"I'm glad you acknowledged our three-way chemistry," I said, "I feel it too. It's extremely potent!" The Phoebe Bridgers album cover was displayed onto the TV screen in front of us, and the speakers projected her billowing electric guitar notes and lyrical vocals. "And it's not something I can ignore, now that we're talking about it. So yes, I'm open to it." I wasn't lying, but I was deliberately omitting the complex feelings behind the whole truth.

"Good!" Sophia said. "Because that's something I'd be excited to explore."

Two days later, Sophia and I went to the gym again, and met Don at his and my place for takeout. I was happy to have time alone with Sophia, and then, to add Don's energy into the mix.

Sophia sat in between Don and me on the couch under a wool blanket. Don tapped on his phone to change the lighting scene to *spring flowers* and our floor lamps bathed the room in shades of pink and warm white. Sophia asked me if she could kiss Don. My whole body buzzed with a yes. I liked knowing that kissing would be all we'd do that night.

At dinner, I'd expressed my desire to take things slow. I didn't want to jump into sex and lose myself in the intensity. "I like to be made to wait," Sophia replied smiling. She had a way of seeming like she was both very open and holding something back at once. There was a mysteriousness about her that was enthralling, that made Don and me want to chase her.

Don and I had a few family and work trips in a row, and Sophia was in a report card crunch at school before leading a student trip to Boston. This made our longing for each other even stronger. We were only able to see her once every couple of weeks. We sent messages every day in a group text chain.

**SOPHIA**

I dreamt about you two last night and woke up touching myself which has never happened before.

**DON**

That's very nice. When we had sex last night, we talked about you and imagined you were with us.

**SOPHIA**

How did it feel? To imagine me with you?

**ALEX**

I came very quickly and very hard, and I was excited, smiling big, and felt extra affectionate and loving towards Don.

**SOPHIA**

That's so nice!!

**ALEX**

D felt expansive, and extra warm towards me, and excited to feel the heightened sensations we all felt when we were together.

### triad / triptych

**SOPHIA**

I have a desire, I think awakened by time at
the gym with A, that the three of us go to a
fancy spa where we can be in the same room
for massages and I can covertly watch the
two of you being tended to and know my own
skin is getting ready to be near yours.

> **ALEX**
>
> This is sexy and sounds wonderful. Doing this
> outside the city and being in nature at the
> same time would be lovely.

**SOPHIA**

Yes! We could go hiking.

> **ALEX**
>
> D hates hiking but I loooove hiking. He could
> get some downtime while you and I go explore
> the woods.

Don and I drove home from a trip to see my family in Montreal.
I was driving, trying to keep both hands on the wheel, when Sophia sent us pictures of her trying on a bra with delicate gray lace
and a sheer cup. Don read me her texts and described the picture.

I had never experienced simultaneous arousal and fear like I
did on that car ride. Sophia had become the center of my every
conversation with Don. This three-way infatuation shattered the
vision of polyamory that I had; even when I was with Lukas and

we were dreaming of a vacation in Spain, or other projects for the future, Don was my *anchor*. I was able to navigate the world living in a pair like everyone else. It's as if I'd imagined a traditional love life with a twist. When Don and I crushed on the same person *together*, it cracked that framework completely open.

After seeing Sophia for a couple of months, a few days passed without her replying to our text messages. When she resurfaced, she told us she was in the middle of a breakup with her live-in partner. They'd been together for eight years. I read Sophia's text aloud at the dinner table, while Don twisted the corner of a paper towel and cleaned one of the intake holes of his e-cigarette.

> I don't want to lose this thing I have with the
> two of you. So I'd like to take a break for a
> little while and come back to you so I don't
> associate time with you with volatility. Will you
> have me then?

We saw Sophia a few more times platonically. I welcomed the respite from the intensity of our triad: the drunken feeling of overwhelming infatuation, the thrill and terror that these intense feelings might cause me to reshape my life completely after just a few dates, the inability to fall asleep without masturbating first—and checking to see if she'd texted.

Our meetings slowed to a drip.

When summer arrived, while Sophia was on a two-week trip in Brazil, she sent us a text letting us know she'd be headed to Argentina for the rest of the summer. We never saw her again.

Sophia disappeared from our life as quickly as she overtook it. It was a *feu de paille*, as we say in French, a straw fire—catching suddenly, burning hot and high, and going out as quickly, leaving cold ashes.

## III. Aly

Aly and I sat on either side of Don on the couch, each resting our head on one of his shoulders. Casino squeezed herself in between my hip and the armrest, and rested her head on my thigh. The light sculpture illuminated the living room in a diffused pattern of small geometric shapes as we watched *Professor Marston & The Wonder Women*, but I wasn't looking at the screen. I was looking at my hand resting on Don's chest, one inch from Aly's. By the time the Professor, his wife, and their partner finally move in together after consummating their triad, it was clear to me that we were watching a version of the future that we might create. Aly wore a sweater with "flawless" printed in pink capital letters across the front, and the light from the sculpture shimmered on her gold nose ring. I wondered what she was feeling, watching these scenes. Was her heart beating as fast as mine?

The afternoon after Don kicked his mother out for her biphobic comments about me, the day after the Thanksgiving dinner that Aly took part in, I met Aly at her place to debrief. We walked two blocks down on her busy boulevard, and Aly pulled Casino away from a chicken wing bone laying on the ground. We turned on a

side street, walked past a playground with a red and blue structure, and entered an empty basketball court. The afternoon was
cold and windy, and the sky was heavy; weather that suited my
dejection.

"I knew the polyamory part would be challenging for Don's
mom," I said, "but not the queer part. Like, I assumed she'd think
'well queerness isn't a choice, but polyamory is a life you choose
to lead.' Sure, I've known that many people think bisexuality isn't
real—"

"Mm-hmm!" Aly exclaimed, nodding energetically, her black
beanie pompom shaking on top of her head. I knew I didn't need
to elaborate. She'd experienced the same struggles as me.

We watched Casino, running around the basketball court, red
frisbee hanging from her mouth. I chased her for a moment,
jumping towards her to make her run in the opposite direction.
She was a ball of unconditional love, and playing with her lifted
my spirits. I walked back to Aly.

"Do you think that being polyamorous is a lifestyle choice
for you," I asked Aly, out of breath, "or that it's part of your
identity?"

She bent down to pick up the wet frisbee that Casino finally
dropped, and threw it to the other side of the court. It hit the
chain link fence and flopped onto the concrete.

"I don't know," she replied, pensive.

"I mean," I said, "do you think you could go back to monogamy?"

"Sure," she replied, her back turned to me, walking towards
Casino.

Her response surprised me. Did her recent breakup with Jake
poison all polyamorous relationships for her? Would she prefer

monogamy with Don if it was an option? Would she one day find a wife, and break up with us to return to monogamy?

Aly continued—while prying Casino's mouth open to remove a piece of plastic she'd found in the pile of leaves along the fence line—"But not without being utterly miserable."

I laughed in relief. She laughed with me. It often happened, that I missed Aly's sarcasm.

"You?" she asked.

"Oh, I could *never* go back," I said. "The only reason I can conceive spending a lifetime with people now is because it doesn't have to be with just one person."

Aly nodded. "My relationship with the two of you is the first time I'm not keeping an eye on where the exit door is."

My heart bloomed. She'd said *the two of you.*

Aly and I sat on the emerald loveseat in my reading nook, a tiny room that the previous owners used as a walk-in closet. There was wallpaper in every single room of the house, but the one in my nook was the only one I liked: dark red with small white and blue flowers. I would have never chosen it myself, but it made it cozy. Aly wrote her morning pages in a spiral bound notebook, and I read a collection of personal essays written by gardeners. Aly's feet rested on the round coffee table. *Texas* was written in capital letters on her thick wool socks, which were in the state's flag colors. It was March, but my room had no heating vent and remained cold.

"Arielle is coming in May," Aly said, putting her pen down. "And school will be over then, so I'm going to request time off."

"Great!" I said, and closed my book. "I was thinking Province-town?" I was glad she was finally ready to plan our getaway together.

She took a slow breath in, opened her mouth, closed it, and quietly exhaled.

I realized my mistake. "Oh, you meant you'll take your whole vacation to be with Arielle."

"Yeah," she said. She looked down and removed a black dog hair from her white sweatpants.

A wave of disappointment pitched in my stomach, but I tried to keep the pangs in check. I tried to reason with myself: Aly lived with me part time, but she rarely saw Arielle. It made sense that she wanted to spend her time off with her other partner. If I let my feelings get hurt, would I be acting like her ex, spraying her with guilt, even though she'd done nothing wrong. Although... if I did let myself feel disappointed, would it be justified? We'd been talking about planning a vacation together for *months*, and every time I brought it up, she said she'd look at her schedule and get back to me.

**Alex Alberto <alex.alberto@email.com>**

Feb 9, 2022, 8:34am

to Aly, Don ▾

This firm specializes in New York family law.

https://jessicadavislaw.com

My friend Lisa had a 30-min consult with them and said they gave them tons of options and ways to go (Lisa was looking for legal ways to handle a non-traditional co-parenting situation with three parents).

BTW, the website mentions poly families, and LGBTQ.

---

**Aly Tadros <aly.tadros@email.com>**

Feb 10, 2022, 11:04am

to me, Don ▾

Alex! I wanted to respond to this more thoughtfully, while I wasn't in the car.

Thanks for finding this. Jessica should be great and her firm was totally who came to mind for when we want to explore our legal options. That being said, the thought of having that conversation right now is a bit overwhelming. Admittedly, I'm feeling a little tapped, between dealing with the dissolving my domestic partnership with Jake today and getting accustomed to the back & forth between the upstate farm, and work and school in the city. I'm also feeling more of that struggle of wanting to be in two places at once, up at the farm in our cocoon, and down here, rebuilding a sense of independence & nurturing friendships. I know you found this to try to take care of me (because you are thoughtful like that) and were only suggesting we have a consultation to find out about the possibilities (and I'm even the one who said I needed/wanted to find legal ways to connect us at some point), but I'm still settling into all the big changes.

So, to be clear: Totally into this, but I'm still very much healing, and need more time. (I'm articulating this for myself as much as I am for you two.)

Make sense?

---

**Alex Alberto <alex.alberto@email.com>**

Feb 11, 2022, 7:02am

to Aly, Don ▾

It absolutely makes sense! Thank you for being open and honest about your feelings (that's one of the things I love about you).

It's helpful to hear. There is no rush whatsoever on this. You're right, I looked it up mostly because I constantly worry that you don't feel equal in our triad because of the weight that the line between Don and I has (being legally married, owning the house, etc.). And since you had mentioned wanting something legal at some point, I wanted to show you that I have no resistance whatsoever to that, on the contrary.

I'm also aware that the relationship between you and me is still young and evolving, and I think you know this but I want to say it: there is no pressure for it to be anything but what it wants to be/what you want it to be, and if you decide that you want to focus more on increasing ties with Don but not going into a full triad integration, that's okay too. I just don't want you to feel pressure to go in a certain direction with the three of us in order to stay in our life, at the farm, etc. Of course we'll always have a partnership and a relationship, but I'm saying this because I want to stress that there are no conditions for you to be a part of our life. No pressure on the amount of time to stay here vs the city, what we call our relationships, even legal entanglement (if you ended up deciding it's not something that you want).

So, let's put this on the back burner and see how things settle. I know you have a lot on your plate, and thank you for coming back to meet my mom this weekend. I know you're swamped and it means so much to me.

---

**Don Thompson <don.thompson@email.com>**

Feb 11, 2022, 10:01am

to me, Aly ▾

I love everything on this thread. I'm enjoying watching Alex do what they always have (I say I want/need something, they spring into action to make it real), and Aly showing her ability to express her feelings/thoughts/needs. It was good for me to see that Alex has no hesitation about pulling the trigger, and I'm glad that Aly got to experience that "speak a need and get a pathway to meeting it within 2 weeks" approach that has served us well for years. It seems like everyone has gotten what they need from this for now, and that makes me happy.

"Casino hears your voice and is wagging her tail," Aly said on my computer screen, tilting her laptop camera towards the floor so Casino entered the FaceTime frame with her tongue out. Aly sat on her couch, in front of her indigo wall. She'd moved since I painted her studio two years prior, but she liked the color and replicated the same accent wall in her new place.

Aly was in her apartment in the city, and I was at the farm Upstate. She was supposed to come up to the farm that weekend, but she'd been closely exposed to Covid. I sat on the loveseat in my reading nook, where Aly and I had talked about her vacation time over two months prior. A warm late-June breeze blew in through the window.

"I've had this pit in my stomach all week," Aly said, "because I'm not sure what it is you want to say."

"I know," I replied. "I felt bad mentioning something serious was coming on an audio note. I didn't want to make your week shittier, but I also didn't want to lie to you and say *no, your intuition is wrong, everything is good.* I've been trying to bring this up for a month, but I always find an excuse not to do it because it always seems like I'll be piling on one more thing on your already overflowing plate, and I know your emotional bandwidth is limited. I thought *I'll wait after her semester is finished,* then *I'll wait until Arielle is gone because I don't want to upset her before she arrives,* then *I'll wait after the shitshow at her office passed, I'll wait after her race.*"

Aly's cat's gray tail poked in and out of the screen.

"I know my life is hectic, but it doesn't mean you can't bring up your needs." Her voice was soft, and I heard a hint of trembling.

"I know. I know," I said, feeling my pulse in my throat. "It's just hard to feel like there's room. So. Um." I moved my computer from my lap to the coffee table and folded my legs under me.

"I've been feeling like there is a gap between how we describe our relationship, and what our relationship actually is," I said.

"Like, we go around and introduce each other as partners, but it no longer feels true."

Aly inhaled and nodded slowly. Her facial expression was hard to read through the slightly pixelated screen.

"I appreciate you bringing this up," she said. "I've felt that shift too, and I've been avoiding thinking about it too much."

I felt a tinge of relief. The weight compressing my lungs eased. My eyes ran across my bookcase in front of my loveseat, then went back to the screen. "Do you remember when you were upset because you felt accessory to Finley's life?" I asked. "So, you were telling me how it seemed like they prioritized their other partner, and saw you as an escape, and all of a sudden it came to me: *I* feel accessory to *your* life. It's like, you *say* you want to be family, and that you want to live here, and you want to be partners, but I don't feel your energy directed towards me, and us. It feels like the times you turn your focus back to me is when something distressing is happening, like when something happened with Arielle on your vacation and you changed your plans last minute to come to the farm and you said all you wanted was to be in our cocoon."

Aly pulled at the corner of her eyes with the tip of her fingers. "It hurts to hear," she said, "because you're so *so* so important to me."

"I know I am. But I guess it doesn't mean that in day-to-day life I'm feeling it? We've talked about this before, but I don't feel like anything has changed. I still feel like I'm at the bottom of the list of everything else in your life. And I don't want to tell you not to train for a race, or not to go on new dates, or not to do your grad school homework, or not to see Arielle, or to find a job that's less taxing for you... but any time you have a sliver of free time, I feel like you redirect it elsewhere."

"I don't want to seem like I'm keeping stock," she said gently. She closed her lips, then parted them. She looked somewhere above the camera for a second. "But I did come up to meet your mom, and it was a lot for me to fit that in my schedule, rent a car, drive up. I was happy to, because I love you, but that was definitely me making you a priority."

"I know, and I loved that you made time for this. But it still feels like the balance of it doesn't add up. I think I'm in the place where I want to transition back to being friends and metamours, with less cohabitation. I know we all said we've always wanted to build tiny cabins so we each have our own space, but it'll be a few years before we can do that, and right now, with everyone in the house... I've started to develop resentment."

For a moment, we both looked at our cameras and said nothing. Her eyes were red and puffy. She looked off screen and petted Casino. Or maybe one of her cats.

"Oh and I want to say," I added, "I'm speaking just for me. You and Don can figure out your relationship from there. I don't want my decision to affect that. I already told him if it means he goes to the city more often to be with you, or that I go to the city more to give you time together at the farm and reduce cohabitation, I'm super supportive of that."

"I don't know what to say," Aly said. Casino appeared on the screen, lifting her paw and putting it on Aly's arm. Casino always did that when she wanted to give us love. "I'm going to need time to process. I just... can't figure out how to make it all work"

"But... have you been happy the way things are?" I asked. "If *I* was happy, would you want to carry on and not change anything?"

Aly's breathing quickened, her chest shaking with sobs. She

closed her eyes and exhaled slowly, then reopened them. "I hear everything you're saying," she said in a small voice, "and even if it hurts, I'm grateful that you're saying it, because I have a hard time admitting these things to myself, and I would have kept avoiding it, but of course you wouldn't, because that's who you are, and that's one of reasons I love you."

I slid into bed. Don took my weighted blanket from the foot of the bed and unfolded it to cover me. I shifted my hips to the left to give him room to sit on the edge of the mattress beside me. A fly buzzed around the lamp on my nightstand, and I considered picking up my swatter, but my limbs were heavy. He put his hand on my sternum, and I took a deep breath.

"I started to think that maybe I've been delusional," I said, "and this whole time what Aly really wanted was to have a close relationship with you, but since I came with you she tried her best to make it work."

"That's not true," Don said tenderly. "I know for a fact that that's not true."

"I can't believe my life looks like this now," I said.

"Like what?" He asked in a low voice.

"Like… so monogamous looking. A couple living in the country in a house on their own. It's just… Aly was here when we moved in, when we thought of the future. We started this *with* her."

"I know," he said, "but more people will come. It won't be like that forever."

The week after my FaceTime conversation with Aly, she and Don did their own relationship check-in.

*I realized that you and Alex aren't it for me,* she'd told him. *It's so close to what I wanted, I think, but not it.*

I raised my hand to play with Don's beard, and looked up at the fly, now buzzing around the ceiling.

"It's hard for two people to have chemistry, imagine three, or more!" I said. "Plus, it has to be someone who wants to live in the country, probably works remotely at first so they *can* live here, also have their shit figured out. It'll never happen."

"Life is very long," Don replied. My finger was still twined in his beard. He often says that.

In the cold depths of the Catskills in February, the winter before Don's and my breakup with Aly, we ran out of oil for the furnace. We'd been living in our new poorly insulated 1860's farmhouse for three months. I slept the night in the upstairs bedroom, wearing thermal underwear, a bright orange beanie and wool socks, under four layers of blankets. I even took out the lime twin-size comforter with pink hearts that my sister used as a kid. Aly and Don slept in the downstairs bedroom together.

I read in bed in the early morning, the cold tips of my fingers out of the covers to hold my book. Daylight gradually peeked through the sides of my bedroom blinds. After I heard the toilet flush, steps and floor planks cracking on the ground floor, I walked downstairs, for once grateful for the gold 70s shaggy carpet covering the hallway. I opened the bedroom door.

"Morning!" Aly said, her gray beanie laying low on her forehead. She pulled the blanket up, inviting me to join in her and Don's warmth.

As soon as I slid in under the covers, Casino jumped from the floor onto the bed, putting all of her eighty pounds on my abdomen to reach a narrow space in between Aly and me, her head at our knees, her tail in Aly's face. Don, on the other side of the bed, crossed his arm over Aly to scratch Casino's ears. Casino was always the happiest when the three of us were in the same room.

"It looks like her tail is your mustache," I told Aly.

Aly held Casino's tail above her lip and wiggled her shoulders. "Ello, mademoiselle," she said, in an exaggerated French accent.

We both laughed uncontrollably, a case of the morning giggles. The eastern sun shone on Aly's dark freckles, and this was the warmest I'd been in days, maybe years.

# relationship advice from your polyamorous friend

Hi, it's me; your one polyamorous friend. No, not the swinger who goes to masked sex parties once a season, or the one secretly cheating on their partner. The one who's managed to balance as many as three relationships at a time for the past ten years with the skill of a Saturday brunch server in the East Village. The *polyamorous* one. Polyamory is about developing multiple relationships with partners that you care about, with everyone in the know and—in my case—everyone hanging out with each other. For me, it's not about casual sex. *Amor* means love!

What qualifies me to give you love advice, you ask? Well, for one, people ask me for it. Plus, I read, think, and write a lot about love. Am I an expert? Can anyone be an expert in love? Who knows. But I try to stay light on the advice part of my responses; I think it's more useful for me to pose questions. I also share my own personal experiences; you decide how or if they're relevant to you.

I don't think polyamory is superior to monogamy. Monogamy is a perfectly great relationship model. And my way of doing polyamory is not the *one right way* to do non-monogamy. I hate the *poly-er than thou* crowd. But I keep hearing that my perspective on relationship challenges is unique because of my non-traditional way of looking at love, so maybe monogamous folks could learn something from polyamorous experiences like mine.

Here are some real questions from people in my life. I hope that you find it useful.

–Your polyamorous friend (34, they/them)

Dear Polyamorous Friend,

My boyfriend is sweet, outgoing, creative and super handy. We've been dating for four years, but we live an hour and a half apart. I love how he keeps me grounded and encourages me, and I've helped him communicate his emotions better. We have no serious issues. So we should move in together, right?

When we started talking about the future, he said his dream would be to build his own cabin on my land, behind my house, so he could continue to have his "space." It confused me. For him, "moving in" means moving into my backyard?

I'm starting to think he's afraid of commitment. Or maybe our relationship isn't what I thought it was. Or maybe I'm overreacting. I wonder if I'm afraid of not living in the same building because that's what I *want*, or because it's what I have always envisioned for myself, and what I see other people doing?

–Home Sweet Home Apart (26, she/her)

Dear HSHA,

I love that you're already trying to investigate the difference between what you may need and what has been programmed in you—for example, the notion that true love equals living together under the same roof. You may have heard of the *relationship escalator*: It's a metaphor for the ways we've been conditioned to think about relationship goals from the minute we start liking someone. To "ascend" from exclusivity, to moving in together, to getting married (and pushing our friendships to the backseat), to raising kids.

On my first date with Don, my partner of eight years, I told him I'd been exploring non-monogamy since I'd moved from Montreal to New York City a few years earlier. I explained to him that it was something I needed to be happy. He said he was open to it, and added that there was also something *he* needed: he couldn't imagine himself living full time with anyone, even in a future committed long-term relationship. For him, full-time cohabitation felt claustrophobic. He wanted to know that if he was having a rough day or feeling particularly introverted, he didn't *have* to be his usual kind, thoughtful, emotionally available self with a cohabiting partner. It occurred to me then that I'd questioned monogamy, but never co-living. I was still early in my journey.

For the first few years of our relationship, Don and I spent four days a week in the same space (and rented out the other one on Airbnb when it was empty). To my surprise, I liked having my own space! However, it didn't feel right to say, "my place" and "his place." I wanted to be able to talk about the two places in ways that reinforced our long-term commitment to one another. So, we started referring to our apartments by the name of the street they were on: "I'm coming to 116th after work." We were building a home *together*, we just had the extreme privilege of spreading our home across two apartments.

When Don started snoring, I tried to use a white noise machine to cover it up, but it wasn't enough to keep me asleep through his guttural noises. I bought special earbuds made for sleeping, and the sound of crashing waves mostly absorbed the snoring, but I woke several times a night with the urge to pee.

Oh, but the nights Don spent with his other partner were amazing! My dreams were uninterrupted, I slept like a starfish in the middle of the bed, I fell asleep to audiobooks playing on my phone, I could eat a granola bar in the middle of the night without worrying about the crackling paper.

When Don and I moved to the country in Upstate New York, not only did we keep a small apartment in the city, but we also planned to each have our own bedroom in the farmhouse. I loved being able to choose the art that

*I* wanted on my walls without having to consider his
preferences. The sketch of a naked woman wearing a
masquerade mask I bought from a street artist in New
Orleans hangs where I'm certain Don would have wanted
to put his print by some sixteenth century painter obsessed with the apocalypse. I love not having to tiptoe
when I wake up at farmer time, hours before any of my
partners. My early morning moans about the state of the
world as I read the news in bed can be as loud as they
need to be.

Still, for the first few months, I felt uneasy about what
it *meant* to no longer sleep in the same bed as Don. Did it
mean our love wasn't as strong as it once was? Would we
slowly become detached and eventually break up? If
people found out we no longer slept together, would they
worry?

We were as emotionally intimate—and felt as fulfilled
in our relationship—as we had ever been. More, maybe.
We cuddled regularly under the covers; we made steady
progress towards our long-term goals for our community
farm. I still told Don he had the softest cheekbones and
he still told me I had beautiful big teeth (he has always
had a weakness for toothy smiles). Old bedtime routines
were updated and reinvigorated with new ones that were
more purposeful about keeping our connection strong.

Even though I was years into my polyamorous journey and had already discarded so many societal expectations of love, I still had to do serious inner work to
deprogram the belief that people who love each other
must sleep in the same bed. Once I was able to let that

belief go, I discovered something about myself that still surprises me sometimes: I'm someone who prefers sleeping alone.

Many nights, when Don tucks me in, I spread my arms and legs as far as I can and feel a giggle of pleasure at the night ahead in my big bed, all alone. I control its temperature, I flop around with abandon, and not a single thought arises about anyone else's sleep all night. Soon after this solo-sleeping revelation, a first date told me that, although she liked to nap with a partner, she couldn't sleep an entire night in the same bed with anyone. She said it delicately, with a tinge of embarrassment, like it might be a deal breaker—or at least a letdown—for me. But I was overjoyed. It wasn't just me!

Is sharing a roof with your boyfriend something that you *need* (that he may not be able to give you), or are you afraid of what others will think? Are you jumping to conclusions about what this may mean for your relationship? I suggest breaking down what you want into the smallest possible negotiation units; by wanting to live together, do you mean sleeping in the same bed (and if so, does it need to be every night of the week, or some/most nights)? Cooking together? Sharing finances? Splitting household chores? And what do you need in order to feel secure in your relationship? Scheduled quality time, loving compliments, spontaneous kisses? Once you have a general idea of what's important to you, ask your boyfriend to do the same: What needs is he trying to address with this proposed cabin? There may be ways to make sure both of you have your needs fulfilled, whether it's his alone time or your feeling of commitment in day-to-day life.

Imagine you could design your relationship with Legos: you can pick the pieces you want, leave aside the ones you don't, and build any shape you like. Pieces could represent any aspect of a relationship: traveling together, having sex, cuddling and kissing, co-parenting children, co-parenting animals, marriage or alternative legal ways of binding yourselves to one another (will, power of attorney, domestic partnership). Some people use a smorgasbord analogy instead of the Lego one, but Legos feel safer to me because I've always worried about germs at buffets.

∞Love,

Your Polyamorous Friend

Dear Polyamorous Friend,

I've been with my girlfriend for six months. I'm head over heels for her. She helped me do so much healing.

I don't know how to tell her that I'm still friends with my ex, Joanne. Joanne and I talk every few weeks. We had dinner together last week, the first time since my girlfriend and I have been together. I'm not in love with Joanne anymore, but her friendship is important to me. I particularly like sharing food with her; my girlfriend is amazing, but she doesn't appreciate good food and wine like I do. Joanne and I connected around cooking and it's something I've missed in my life. Should I try to explain all this to my girlfriend or cut ties with Joanne? I haven't been this happy in a relationship in a long time, and I don't want to jeopardize it.

–Trying Not to Mess Up (41, she/her)

Hi Trying,

I'm curious about why you are concerned about disclosing your ongoing contact with Joanne to your current girlfriend. Has she explicitly shared a "no exes policy?" Have you had jealous girlfriends in the past?

I know dealing with exes is something that can be delicate, and there's potential for difficult emotions, so I don't mean to trivialize your challenge. My intention is to interrogate the underlying assumptions that are leading you to feel conflicted—and to act in a way that feels dishonest to you. Often, we avoid direct conversations about expectations with new partners because we either believe that we can intuit our partner's stance on everything, from how important birthdays are to ex-girlfriend policies, or because we are afraid that their stance will conflict with our own. When we avoid those conversations, we instead operate from *presumed* agreements.

In monogamous relationships, we tend to assume our partner will fill every single one of our needs, and we try to do the same. But that's a lot of pressure to put on one person. One of the benefits of polyamory is that we relieve our partners of that pressure (and in turn, we are relieved of it, too). In polyamory, that means that no one partner is expected to meet all of your romantic and sexual needs.

Your romantic partner cannot possibly meet all of your social and emotional needs, which is why close platonic friendships outside of romantic partnerships are healthy.

I hate tennis, but my partner Don loves playing, so once he found a tennis partner, I was thrilled that he no longer hassled me to buy a racket. I love hiking, but Don calls it "walking for no reason," so I do it with other partners and friends.

Don feels big and protective to me and makes me feel "little" (in comparison) and cared for. He helps me get in touch with my childlike sense of wonder. In contrast, my last girlfriend made me feel big and strong, and saw my gender queerness like no one else. I don't consider myself particularly funny in most areas of my life, but once or twice a year when I get together with a former partner of mine from my hometown, I make him laugh like no one else.

In your case, it seems like sharing an intimate relationship with food is something that your girlfriend isn't interested in, but that Joanne is.

What exactly do you want your relationship with Joanne to look like? How often do you want to see her? Do you want to be able to exchange friendly touch, like a hand on a shoulder or tight hugs? You should also ask

Joanne what *she* wants out of her relationship with you, too. It would be helpful if, when you tell your girlfriend about it, you're able to explain how you envision your relationship with your ex, so she can understand it and let you know what she feels comfortable with.

If you ask your girlfriend to trust you, you need to make sure that you can uphold your commitments to her. Do you feel like your relationship with your ex is in a solid platonic friendship place, and your feelings for her are sorted and won't affect your new relationship? Do you have a history of breaking commitments or being unfaithful to partners that your girlfriend is aware of? Does she have any reason to be untrusting?

Either way, omitting the fact that you've had dinner with your ex has the potential to create distrust in your relationship. So I suggest you have an honest conversation sooner than later and define what you expect in your relationships with everyone else, not just exes. What does monogamy mean for you two? Different people draw the line in different places: for some, it means never even *thinking* about anyone else sexually, and foregoing masturbation and porn. For others, flirting is okay as long as nothing physical happens. Some allow emotional intimacy with others as long as it doesn't become physical. Hopefully you and your girlfriend can get on the same page and move forward with an agreement that works for you both.

∞Love,
Your Polyamorous Friend

Dear Polyamorous Friend,

My boyfriend of seven years—with whom I bought the perfect house two years ago—wants to break up with me because our sex life began to gradually vanish four years ago. He now sees me only as his best friend. We have tried some things together to heal our intimacy in the last few years, but they did not feel right, so we stopped. Now he feels like his sexual desire for me will never return. I also wonder if my desire for him will ever come back.

The problem is that I cannot imagine my life without him in it. I love him so much! He is my favorite person in the world! We cook together, play board games, laugh, and take care of our beautiful furry babies.

Should I press him to continue trying to reignite our sexual and romantic flame? Should I let him go? But how can I let my best friend go?

–Eternal Lover (32, she/her)

Hi EL,

Let me ask you this: What are the parts of your relationship that still work and fulfill both of you? It sounds like cohabitating, raising animals, and being friends are aspects that make you happy. Does he feel the same way?

Heteronormative (and mononormative) culture has taught us that relationships have to be all or nothing. That if you no longer have sex and don't feel a certain kind of romantic love, you need to let go of that person entirely. But what if, instead of a capital B breakup, you explored the possibility of a *relationship transition*?

The expectations that you and your boyfriend have had for one another are no longer met, and holding onto those expectations causes you suffering. What if you had the opportunity to build something new: a new relationship structure with different expectations? Can you envision being best friends and roommates? Or maybe you can't imagine continuing to live together, but you can see a future in which you remain close and still share in the caring of your pets. Perhaps you have common projects or hobbies that you'd like to continue enjoying together (game nights?), while giving each other room to find another partner that will give you the kind of romance you no longer have for each other.

Two years ago, my partner, Aly, and I made a commitment to create a home together with Don. We did not yet live together full time; I lived in Upstate New York on the farm and site of our future joint home, and she split her time between New York City and Upstate. A year in, I felt Aly's energy becoming scattered. Rather than spend her time off working and playing at the farm, she spent it with another partner in the city. When her professor canceled a class on a Thursday, she took the opportunity to schedule a first date, rather than a long weekend with us. She prioritized races, new dates, school and work.

Individually, I supported all these things, but collectively they left no room for us. I brought my feelings up in several conversations, and she continued to say she wanted to build a home and a family with us Upstate. Her actions continued to show otherwise.

I had months of stomach churning before I was able to tell her that I felt like we should change the way we viewed our relationship and our future together. I was scared I'd hurt her, and I did not want to lose her. But I was already grieving what our relationship had been, and what I thought our future would be together.

When we finally had space for the conversation, she sobbed, barely able to catch her breath. She'd felt the shift in our relationship too but had been avoiding admitting it to herself. She appreciated that I initiated the check-in. She called me the *canary in the coal mine that is our relationship*; she and Don can let issues stagnate for a long time before addressing them.

Even though we were all experienced with polyamory, we had made a big mistake when we merged our lives: we didn't intentionally *design* our relationship. We didn't discuss what *triad* meant for each of us. We didn't talk about what "building a home together," really meant in practice, or about each other's expectations and needs. We blindly slid into a domestic life because it felt so good and natural. For a time.

Aly realized that, as much as she wanted our farm—and Don and me—to be her home, it wasn't quite right for her. But, we both wanted to stay in each other's life. We're both memoirists, and we continue to support each other with our writing (she's helped me edit this entire book, line by line). This is still one of the most special parts of our relationship. I expect we'll collaborate on a piece or an anthology together one day, and we have plans to organize writers' retreats. We remain friends and creative partners, and we may be business partners in the future. She visits Upstate sometimes, and I see her when I travel to New York City. We all know that we can count on one another in emergencies. But we no longer have plans to build a home or live together. We did need to take a bit of a step back at first so we could each process and grieve this other kind of future we thought we'd be building together, but then, slowly, we started to reshape our relationship.

Now, I'm not saying that this kind of transition is for everyone and every relationship. Sometimes people do need to get out of each other's lives, or spend some time apart before they are ready to build something different. Some people can't imagine remaining platonically close and risk seeing each other fall in love with someone new. I don't know if you're that type of person, but you should get to uncouple in the way that *you* (and your partner) want. The first step is figuring out what that is.

∞Love,

–Your Polyamorous Friend

# people ask

## But, did you and Aly have sex?

The summer Aly and I made the decision to transition out of our life partnership, I avoided the brightness of the sun. It was my first season on our new Catskills land. When I worked on the farm in the Hudson Valley the year prior, I spent all of my free time outside: I ate breakfast on the stone patio in my underwear, I hiked every weekend, I dipped in swimming holes and watched sunlight pierce the cold water and lick my naked thighs. But that summer following my breakup with Aly, I was constantly exhausted. I felt disoriented and spent a lot of time inside. How had I ended up living in a farmhouse in the country as half of a hetero and monogamous-passing couple?

The day we got the keys to our new house, just seven months earlier, Aly stood in our kitchen with Don and me, toasting this long-awaited step with non-alcoholic champagne. She and I hauled the previous owners' flower patterned couches into a pickup truck to take to the dump. She cooked moussaka in our small toaster oven because the big one did not work. That whole winter, Don, Aly and I sat around the table in the formal dining room most Saturday nights, sharing our personal goals for the coming week, asking how we could support one another.

When we started working with an architect to plan renovations to the farmhouse, the three of us asked ourselves how we needed to design the space to serve our day-to-day.

"I really prefer sleeping alone," I said. "I can sleep with you every once in a while," I told Aly, "but I can't handle Don's snoring. I'm amazed that you can. Plus, I go to bed hours before both of you." They nodded, and I took a sip of my non-alcoholic IPA. "Don, do you think that you'll want your own bedroom?"

"Honestly," Don said, "my room is wherever I sleep that night. As long as I have my magic bag, I'm good."

Don carries all of his essentials in the same black leather computer bag, and has for years. It holds his: laptop, chargers for his phone and e-cigarette, prescription meds and extra nicotine cartridges, wallet, passport, a water bottle, a couple of low sugar protein bars, and Splenda (in case the coffee shop doesn't have it). If Aly or I need a Tylenol, eye drops, or allergy medicine, he has it—hence, the "magic." He carries the bag from room to room as he moves through the house, and wherever he goes. He has a terrible memory, so this system works for him; he never forgets anything important.

I looked at the printed floor plan of the house on the dining table. "Maybe we could add a closet in the hallway in between those two bedrooms for you, Don," I said, tapping my finger on the landing at the top of the stairs "and your clothes could be in it.

That way, if either Aly or I are sleeping or on a call in our rooms, you still have access to your stuff."

Aly laughed. "We'll give him a cart like floaters have in schools."

I bursted out laughing. "Oh my god yes!"

Don's eyes toggled back and forth between Aly and me for a few seconds. "I have no idea what you're talking about," he said.

"You know," I said, still giggling, "teachers who don't have their own classrooms, they push a cart with some books and teaching materials and move from room to room."

Aly and I continued laughing as Don looked at us with an amused smile.

In hindsight, I think the desire I had for a more physical love with Aly was about cuddling, holding hands, kissing, embracing in public. Sensuality between Aly and me involved us pressed against one another, sinking into my plush wool mattress, our skin lightly touching where our bodies were uncovered at the edges of the soft cotton layers of our pajamas; the strip of her warm lower back against my inner forearm, her fingertips on my outer thigh below my gray boxers. It did not extend to opening up our sexual selves to one another, to mixing our fluids, to being fully, physically naked together. I craved holding hands and kissing her in public—but was it because my body wanted it, or because my heart needed to make our deep bond visible to the outside world? To have it expressed in a language people would understand: something that signified romantic and physical love, and therefore important, real, *high priority*. That's what life partners do. That's how partners look.

Aly was in the fabric of the house and the Upstate life we'd built. With Aly and Don, I'd had a family. With just Don, I had a partner. I was in a *couple.* This breakup hit me harder than most of my prior relationships that had involved sex. So no, Aly and I did not have sex, but my heart and my vision of the future were shattered nonetheless.

## Will you look for another third?

I've ended up in a triad with Don three times through serendipity, not because we had been seeking it. Having a woman or gender-queer person included in my relationship with Don makes me feel more complete—all the parts of myself converging together into the same core, as opposed to having parallel relationships that don't intersect.

But every time Don suggests we try to find another mutual partner on dating apps, I feel resistance in my body. There is something icky about "unicorn hunting," even if we try to approach it in a way that invites this third person as an equal part of our relationship, with room for our partnerships to become whatever they're meant to become.

But then I wonder: If a partner of mine moves in and joins me in building a family, wouldn't they also be Don's life partner? Compartmentalizing relationships isn't so easy, especially if I remove sex from the equation.

## Don't you want a family?

It bothers me that people use *family* as a shorthand for *parents and kids.* I do want a family. Just not in the form many might think.

I was five when I told my mother, in between bites of Shake 'n Bake chicken, that I didn't want to birth babies (though then, I thought babies came out of the rear, as I later explained to my parents, aided with a drawing I'd made). "I want to adopt a baby," I said, "but an older baby that no one wants." I'd seen something on TV about adoption and how kids older than one rarely found parents. Even though I didn't know anyone who had been adopted, it was natural for me to understand that we could build a family with existing humans. Maybe the fact that my older half sister and I had different fathers but that I'd always seen her as my *full* sister contributed something.

Throughout my twenties, when I saw babies cooing in strollers or kids laughing in the park I never heard that biological tick. But I felt an internal longing when I watched movies with gray-haired characters who had been friends and neighbors for decades and gathered for dinner several times a week. That intuitive ring grew even louder when it was a group of people who were not blood-related but operated as a tight-knit unit. When that group was intergenerational, it thundered.

**But if you don't want kids, what will you do when you're old?** people then ask. The premise of the question is flawed—children don't always become caregivers for their aging parents. I myself have set down roots five hours from my parents. We are separated by a border that was closed for months during Covid. I visit and help as much as I can, but I'm not providing weekly in-person support as they age.

When I think of family resilience and aging, I think of an intergenerational *chosen* family. That chosen family could include members of a family of origin if one *chooses*, but it's by no means necessary. My chosen family will certainly include younger people and children, just not mine (though the definition of *mine* is elastic). To me, a non-nuclear family is more resilient and has potential for deeper mutual aid and care than the nuclear family.

One of my creeping worries is that I have become too reliant on Don. That my identity and wellbeing are primarily tied to him. Until we grow our family, until we (or I) have one or more other life partner(s), whether they be romantic, sexual, platonic, or some combination, my family feels precarious.

My life experience has made me acutely aware and sensitive to familial vulnerability. My sister's father drowned when she was eleven. My aunt's first husband was a trucker and died in an accident when he was in his early thirties. Both my grandfathers died of heart attacks in their early sixties. My father had a stroke that left him disabled when he was only fifty-one. The planet is on fire. When I think of a resilient future, it necessitates having multiple life partners. I need to know my stool won't get knocked over if one leg breaks.

I still love the idea of being significant in a child's life. I'm sad that my sister's kids grew up far away from me, and I was not able to be that for them.

"If we have a kid, what should they call you?" Hannah asked me when she dropped off Marcy, her adorable pit bull and golden retriever mix, for a long weekend. "Like," she continued, "we were telling Marcy in the car *we're going to see uncle Don and—*" She paused. "And we realized we didn't know how to refer to you."

Hannah and her husband Joe had become close friends of ours. They'd moved from the U.K. a few years prior, and lived in an off-grid cabin nearby.

"Maybe just Alex?" I suggested.

"But we like the idea of having a word that carries a familial meaning. Is there a gender neutral term for aunt and uncle?"

I teared up. The fact that she used the word "familial," to describe our friendship made my heart swell.

"I'm not sure," I replied, swallowing my emotion. "I'll think about it and do some research." She grinned and squeezed my upper arm.

After discarding *pibling* and *parsib* (parent sibling), and *unty* (the pronunciation is too close to "auntie"), I came up with *zuntie*. Zuntie Alex. I imagined their toddler calling me that in a British-American accent and smiled. Two months later, Hannah and Joe would move in with us. This was temporary—the winter in their off-grid cabin was harsher than they'd hoped. We had an extra bedroom in our house, so we offered it to them. We knew Hannah and Joe did not want to build the kind of long-term co-living life we dreamed of, but this experience solidified our relationship as extended family members.

Parents around me are all drained, sleep deprived, and have no time for themselves. I heard Sheila Liming say on The Ezra Klein Show that parents of young children do not have the capacity to give back to their friends. That, until their kids reach their teens, having a friendship with a parent is often a one-way street. Maybe my role in helping raise the next generation isn't to be the primary parent of a child myself, but rather to be a supporter of a handful of parents, and allow them to be better parents to *their* kids. And be the Zuntie who takes little ones out on fun outings and covers a few caregiving shifts each week. To witness their discovery of the world and build additional scaffolding around their growth.

## Polyamory sounds good in theory, but isn't it a lot of work?

I imagine this is similar to telling a parent: "Having kids sounds good in theory, but it sounds like a lot of work!"

Yes. Polyamory is a lot of work. But it also gives me a kind of happiness and purpose that I could never access in a monogamous life. The grunt of the work is because, growing up, most of us are not explicitly taught the kind of communication required for *one* relationship to be successful—imagine the compounding effect of balancing multiple commitments. We have to build new relationship models from scratch. We have to read and educate ourselves, build something against the grain, figure out legal ways that we can navigate the rigid nuclear family system. It can be exhausting.

Don and I went to the first annual AltSex conference in New York City in 2016. Most of the attendees were therapists, but we went because we were starved for education. Dr. Rosalyn Dischiavo gave a presentation about transitions in polyamorous systems, using research conducted with monogamous blended families—in which two adults who had kids in previous unions joined to form a new family. She talked about typical steps that those families go through.

- First, the *Fantasy Stage*: They imagine an idealistic and unrealistic version of what their new family life will be like.

- Second, the *Immersion Stage*: When they merge their lives, family members are confronted with day-to-day challenges and friction, and they realize the fantasy they had wasn't real.

- Third, the *Awareness Stage*: Members actively try to understand how this new family might work.

- Fourth, the *Mobilization Stage*: Members clash, there is conflict, everyone expresses what they need and attempts to meet others' needs.

- Fifth, the *Action Stage*: Members negotiate new agreements and establish a solid foundation for their family.

- Finally, in the *Contact Stage*: The family unit has reached a happy balance, and members form positive emotional bonds.

In a polyamorous system, every time someone new enters or exits, it rocks the whole family unit. The intensity of that rocking depends on how core that person was in the system. It requires effort from all involved to process the emotions that come with the change and find a new balance. Polycules inherently have increased potential for entrances and exits. But as I said earlier, it also has increased potential for resilience and joy.

After Aly left Don and me, I did enjoy the calm and the reduced frequency of delicate family check-ins. The months leading to our breakup had been draining. Don and I had our routines down, and we'd had seven years to hone our one-on-one communication skills. But despite enjoying this simplified day-to-day, I cyclically felt a gaping longing. I knew my family was incomplete.

## Isn't it hard being queer and polyamorous in the country?

When I lived in New York City, going on dates with people open to non-monogamy was surprisingly easy but making friends wasn't. When I lived in Montreal, hanging out in each other's homes and having dinner parties was a weekly affair. But it didn't seem to be part of the lifestyle in New York. Apartments were too small and people in my orbit often lived multiple trains away from one another. It was a culture of going out to eat and drink and made me feel like I couldn't create intimacy with people in the same way I did while socializing around someone's books, spices and picture frames.

A few months after I moved to the city, I organized a Swiss fondue dinner with colleagues from the tech startup I worked at. I didn't let the meager square footage of my studio stop me; I slid my desk in the middle of the narrow room, propped each leg of my square Ikea coffee table on stacks of toilet paper rolls to raise its height, and squeezed eight guests around my improvised dinner table. I taught them how fondue works, and we talked about our personal lives, but none of those colleagues became close friends.

I craved a network of companions who I could invite over for a last-minute movie night, who would want to drive to Montreal with me for a weekend, who would help me carry home a mustard armchair on two trains and a 16-block walk. The only reliable way to make new connections was to go on dates. No one seemed willing to prioritize close, platonic relationships. Building bonds with metamours did give me a feeling of family, but I still lacked a close-knit community. How did people build that once they were done with school?

I attended a few queer meetups, but I suffered from imposter syndrome: I wasn't gay enough. And in large groups of hetero colleagues, I didn't feel straight enough. I tried to join social events for bisexual folks, but wasn't able to make long-lasting connections there either.

Then I moved Upstate.

I sat outside a café, at a picnic table on a warm spring day, when a tall brunette with a septum piercing asked if she could sit next to me. We were both killing time before a new yoga class next door. "My sister is moving to the area soon," Catherine said, "and she's worried about not finding queer community." She looked down for a moment. "I don't want to assume, but..."

I laughed. "Yes, I'm queer."

"Oh good! I've been keeping my new-friend-radar on for a while. I'm also trying to build my community."

She asked me if I wanted to join her for Taco Tuesday at a bar nearby after our class, and we've been friends ever since.

I made dozens of friends that way. Simply. People showed up when I offered to go on a hike, or came over to play Terraforming Mars. Less than a year after I'd moved to the Catskills, I had a strong group of friends. We got together in December for Sinterklaas, a Dutch holiday that connects Hannah to the Netherlands, where she was born. We got together at Easter and painted eggs because Catherine loves it. Twelve of us squeezed in around a small TV to watch the Superbowl even if only Don and Catherine's mom actually like football. When I had a grueling task to do on the farm, I sent a text in our group thread and someone showed up the next day to help out. When I sit in my local coffee shop, at least five different people I know will inevitably come ask me how I'm doing, and *genuinely* want to know the answer. Someone will ask about my chicks. Someone else will ask how my manuscript is progressing.

In *Real Queer America: LGBT Stories from Red States*, Samantha Allen writes of urban centers like San Francisco and New York: "These might be vaunted LGBT hot spots, but they are also exhausting and brutal places to visit, let alone live. The queer communities there can be cliquey, too, because people are spoiled for choice; in red-state oases, I've felt so much more adhesiveness between the L and the G and the B and the T."

New York may be a blue state, but the further you drift from New York City, the redder it gets. Trump and *Fuck Biden* flags are sprinkled throughout my area. People write *go to the city* on Facebook event pages for queer meetups. Someone was refused service at a gas station because they wore a pride shirt. But the community of queer folks and allies is the strongest I've ever had. My experience is consistent with the one described in Allen's book. While life here is by no means perfect, everyone representing the wide range of rainbow letters sticks together. And more broadly, there is a community-level care that I couldn't find in the city. I'm incredibly grateful for my time in New York City—it allowed me to explore my sexuality, identity, and new relationship models in a way that felt safe and anonymous. But while I found myself in the city, I created *home* in the country.

# i ask

## Will I ever want to have sex regularly again?

I don't keep a sex diary, but by my estimation, I haven't had sex more than five times in the past two years. Some people might feel sad for me and think that it's something I should fix. But really, I've been quite happy. I simply seem to have lost the interest, the need, the urge. Maybe my anti-depressants contributed, maybe it's because I've been on this rocky gender journey, maybe I've just been in a season of my life in which sex isn't how I want to connect with people. I've wondered if I was on the asexual spectrum because of how often I've felt intense platonic love for my friends and how satisfied I've been not having sex. But sexual exploration and intimacy were a core part of my life and identity until my early thirties. Could I be asexual despite having been hypersexual for so long? Can one *become* asexual? Can one fluidly move between sexual and asexual?

In her book *Heaven Is a Place On Earth*, Adrian Shirk recounts telling a friend, while high, that her sexuality felt "deeply communal." She wasn't sure what she even meant by that statement, and I wasn't either when I read it, but I instantly knew I felt similarly.

Adrian unpacks what she means: "The erotic can show up in so many forms other than sex," she writes, "and when I thought about my modern fantasy of pre-modern society (bear with me), anywhere in the world, I imagined that the erotic was often found in the goings-on of daily life: growing food, harvesting, hunting, living so close to one another, eating together, seeing each other through ceremony and season."

Here is what I have found erotic: Editing this book, my legs propped on the coffee table, while my creative partner laid on her stomach on the gray rug and highlighted sections of the printed draft of her own book in yellow. Reshaping rocky garden beds with a rake in the 80 degree sun with a new friend while talking about how the nuclear family has fucked everyone over. Crying in front of Hannah in the middle of the coffee shop and not wiping my tears in embarrassment. Don returning from the local thrift store with an orange tie that he thought I'd look handsome wearing. Hannah and Joe coming over Thursday nights for dinner because we want to nurture our deep bond.

When I meet someone who has the potential to become a good friend, that person floods my brain the same way any crush would. I feel a rush of dopamine in the same realm that once accompanied sexual attraction. I have crushes on most of my friends. I fantasize about joint projects: backpacking trips in the mountains, drawing the trail map of my woods, committing to watching a whole season of *Half Bad* together.

I do experience the occasional jolt of sexual attraction, and I'm open to letting myself fall into a more traditionally sexual place with an existing partner, a new partner, or just with myself. But I've stopped feeling like my lack of sexual activity is something I need to fix. Shame is pervasive like that—I used to feel ashamed for having too much sex, then I felt ashamed for not having any. Enough already.

## What even is a "partner?"

When I started writing this book, I thought it would end in a sort of polyamorous *happily-for-a-long-time-after.* And now, I'm desperately wanting to insert someone or someone*s* into my narrative to give you a more satisfying ending, to make my own personal narrative more whole. One that tells you *look, polyamory works and life doesn't have to be anchored around a two-person unit.* There is a void I'm craving to fill—both in the pages of the book you're holding, and in my heart.

I think a lot about the love stories I grew up seeing in books and movies. How most people around me consider a relationship a failure if it ended. But why would the criteria for something's success be that it never ended—or never evolved into something different? I did not *end up* with Aly, but our relationship was—is—beautiful and taught me so much.

People like to define "partner" as someone to climb the relationship escalator with. But I've started to look at romance and friendship as overlapping curves on the same spectrum of love. I see a partner as someone I love, and to whom I have made some sort of intentional commitment. Those partnerships can take any shape.

## How do I invite people to become family and create a home?

While I spent the past decade trying to get off the relationship escalator—deprogram all expectations in relationships and instead co-design something custom with all parties involved—I now find that I crave a sort of "chosen-family escalator." I struggle with figuring out how to invite people to be family when the relationship doesn't look like traditional dating. What are the logical steps, the social scripts? There isn't an app for folks trying to build non-nuclear family or intentional communities (though the folks at Remodeled Love are working on this at the time of writing). There are websites for intentional communities that offer classified sections, but posting there has felt daunting and I'm not sure why.

How do you say: I want you to move in with me and my partner and build a life together, but we're not gonna fuck? There are no social scripts for this kind of "courting." What would a "will you be my family" proposal even look like?

Maybe, in the past, I fought so hard and went into debt living alone in a tiny studio because I didn't feel like I could be my full self while living with someone else. I was scared of any framework or rules that might arise with roommates. But there is a difference between having roommates and *co-living*. I think co-living implies a more intentional commitment to designing a life together.

Roommates are short-term solutions for reducing overhead costs and loneliness. They help make individual life in an atomized capitalist system more bearable. But they are expected to drop off once you find the one person with whom you can reach a sustainable income with which to build a nuclear family. Co-living partners are committed to the collective to which you are a part. They are invested in your success and happiness, as you are to theirs. You're in this together, so the frameworks and rules for living are tailored to the members of the collective, and subject to revision, with sustainability top of mind. That's what I want.

## How do I remain non-hierarchical with everyone?

I've been with Don for nine years. We own a property together. Our finances are completely merged. We are legally married, and while we initially did it so I could get a Green Card, we stayed married after we reached the number of years required for me to keep my citizen status in the U.S.

Even if I approach any new partnership as equal in importance and level of prioritization as my relationship with Don, it will take time for me to reach the kind of interdependence and history I have with him. Our ties are flexible, but incredibly strong.

With Aly, I was so worried that she'd feel secondary; every time she asked for something, I jumped on trying to fill that need, like when I researched an attorney specializing in polyamorous families to draw up papers for legally merging our lives. I told her it would be challenging, but I could eventually consider getting a divorce from Don to even out ties between the three of us. I made sure we'd design the house renovations around her needs and that she'd have equal say. But she still felt as though she'd never have equal status. Some of that was Aly's own stuff, but a lot is about how two long-term existing partners have to be explicit and effortful in making space for someone new. Don and I have learned to live in sync in a way that requires minimal effort, and even if we tried hard to prioritize Aly, it is incredibly difficult for two long-term partners to keep their couple's privilege in check. Society is built for *couples*, and it's a daily struggle to try to live differently.

## Could polyamory be a broader life philosophy that extends beyond romance?

When I began my journey into non-monogamy, I was focused on the freedom of developing sexual and romantic intimacy with multiple people. But in my relationship with Bridget, Don's first serious partner, I discovered metamours could become an anchor for me, and a core part of my family. I've worked to gradually let go of hierarchy in my relationships. And as sex took a backseat in my life, and I grew closer to Aly, I discovered the power of platonic relationships and that the lines between friendship and romance could be blurred.

I now view my whole life through a polyamorous lens. For me, that means approaching all my relationships in the same open, flexible, unscripted way: friendships, romantic relationships, creative partners, fellow farmers, mentors, mentees, etc. It means decentering romance in my life and putting other relationships (including the one with myself) on equal footing.

But it has also made me more collectivist in every area of my life. Polyamory taught me how to share romantic love and sex, which culturally, are the most dangerous things to share. Once I learned how to do that, I started seeing the potential for creating abundance everywhere.

# epilogue

Sign up at alexalberto.com/epilogue, and you'll receive an essay that will bring you up to date on some of the events, themes, and characters portrayed in the book.

# acknowledgments

This is my first book, so I've never written acknowledgements before. I'm surprised by how emotional this experience is: looking across my community with gratitude and seeing all of the ways individuals have contributed to my life's journey and this work. Realizing that I could never list every important person and contribution, that I will inevitably miss someone central, and yet really wanting to try to express my gratitude as best I can to the people who are top of mind at this moment. So here goes.

It is an understatement to say that this book wouldn't exist without you, D. Thank you for repeating that I should and *could* write a book for years before I finally believed you, thank you for approaching our relationship as art, thank you for being the first reader and editor of almost everything, thank you for reminding me to record our conversations (especially those that put me in tears), thank you for creating space in our life that allows me to prioritize my writing, thank you for encouraging me to carve my own path in publishing this book. Thank you for seeing me and loving me as I am, always.

Aly Tadros, thank you for carefully editing this entire book. And thank you for letting me share so much of our relationship in these pages. Thank you for the innumerable hours of voice note exchanges. Thank you for dreaming with me.

Caroline Shannon and K.G. Strayer, thank you for launching this Quilted Press experiment with me, and taking this indie publishing journey alongside me.

Chloe Caldwell, your mentorship, editing, and support has seen this book from its inception to final printing, and it would not be the same without you. You are a constant source of inspiration. I could not be more thrilled to have you as my "creative wife" (in a poly way, obviously). Thank you for sharing your magic with me, and letting me organize it.

To everyone who is featured as a character in this book, thank you.

People who have shared their polyamory publicly, in essays and books, on social media, in your workplaces, at family functions, I'm grateful to you. By spreading awareness and being unapologetic, you made it easier for me to come out.

Hannah Beresford, your comprehensive edits helped me take my manuscript to the next level. Thank you for pushing me to better ground my scenes, and for encouraging restraint that made my essays more powerful.

Rachel Ake, I could not have asked for a better collaboration in designing this book cover. Alison Cnockaert, thank you for the beautiful interiors, and for your patience with the many updates to the manuscript. Both of you have made this book design a work of art.

Adriana Newell, thank you for shooting my author photos. I experienced the best gender-euphoria looking at those pictures.

To everyone who backed the Kickstarter campaign, a thousand thanks. You helped not only me and my Quilted Press collaborators, but many more writers who will see that they *can* put their stories out in the world on their own terms.

Special shoutout to Adeem the Artist. Your music makes me feel seen, and is incredibly healing. It connects Southerness and country music to the joy of queerness.

Robyn Lyn, thank you for becoming a Quilted Press Founding Backer. Strangers like you who take a leap in supporting stories like ours make a huge impact. It seeds magic and spreads hope that becomes a legend for the next author worried that no one will care about their book. We need more literary citizens like you.

Brooke M. Haney, I could not have written this book if, years ago, you hadn't believed in me and my solo play. Without your sup-

# acknowledgments

port, I wouldn't have converted my shame into pride, and I wouldn't have developed my confidence as a storyteller. You are an amazing director, writing partner, friend, and editor. And thank you for serving as a sensitivity reader for this book.

To everyone who came to my shows, back when I was still closeted and performing under a pseudonym, who stayed afterwards to tell me how much you needed to hear my stories, thank you. Every single one of you. You gave me the fuel to write this book.

Candy Schulman, I learned to believe in myself as a writer in your workshops. *The Bobby Pin* is the first essay I was ever proud of.

Debra Lynn Driscoll, thank you for being a gentle guide as I was writing the early versions of *Wide Plank Floors*. It was the hardest essay to write in the entire collection. Your workshop on writing about loss allowed me to face a decade of repressed grief. Thank you for your friendship and healing.

Thanks to my writing quad: Magda Cychowski, Da Young Lisa Park, and McKenzie Schwark. Our workshops were crucial in helping me shape this book and keeping me accountable.

Patricia Fancher, I've never felt so instantly seen by a writing buddy, both in your feedback and in your own essays. Thank you for sharing yourself with me.

Les Poétesses Apparues: Gab, Kate, and Lili, thank you for crafting a bilingual writing circle with me. You continue to help me become more authentically queer in French.

Thanks to the early champions of Quilted Press who provided me with invaluable advice and support: Emily Helk at The Lost Bookshop, Randi Sussman-Kim at LionEyesBooks, Sari Botton at Memoir Land/Oldster, Ryan Rivas at Burrow Press, Michael

# acknowledgments

Wheaton at Autofocus Lit, Alison Bailey at The 3rd Thing, Margot Atwell at Feminist Press, Oriana Leckert at Kickstarter, Kailey Brennan and Brittany Ackerman at Write or Die.

Maman, merci for your unconditional love and acceptance. It allowed me to write this book, and flourish as a person. Thank you for coming to every school play, every improv game, every recital. Thank you for being proud of who I am and the singular life I created for myself. Thank you for saying you always knew I was different, and meaning *unique, beautiful, powerful.*

Laurence, merci d'être ma fan numéro un et d'évoluer à mes côtés.

Saga, thank you for the way you unabashedly championed this book. Thank you for letting me see how my writing went straight to your heart. The way you proudly show everyone who you are—colleagues, acquaintances, strangers—is an inspiration. Thank you for joining my family.

My Stamford Coffee family, I don't even know how to begin to express how grateful I am for you (I'm tearing up as I write this). Julian, Vincent, Emma, Christiaan, Kim, Sal. Thank you for giving me a second home and a "coffice" to write this book. Thank you for getting my decaf Americano ready as soon as you see me through the window. Thank you for letting me soak my sweater in the sink every time I spill something on it. Thank you for treating me as part of the team and letting me stay after hours. Thank you for organizing the best open mic series I've ever taken part in. Having a platform to share my works-in-progress kept me in touch with why I was writing this book and helped me push through. And of course, thank you to everyone who attended the open mics and cheered, laughed, cried at my stories. You all directly contributed to this book.

## Maxime Laliberté (1989-2008)

Max, I often think about how I might owe the life I have to you. Meeting you tipped a path full of dominoes. If, when we were fifteen, you hadn't forced me to watch *Friends* and weird indie movies in their original English versions instead of dubbed, I wouldn't have become bilingual. I wouldn't have considered going to school in New York. I wouldn't have met Don, Bridget, Aly. I wouldn't have written this book.

Our relationship taught me early in life that the line between friendship and romance isn't as stark as we think. Our weird love that was sometimes physical left me confused, because you thought you were gay and I thought I was a girl. But now I realize that maybe you were the first person who saw me for who I truly was.

Alex Alberto is a queer and polyamorous storyteller and educator. They grew up in Montreal and currently live in Upstate New York. Their essays have been published in Huffington Post, Write or Die Magazine, and elsewhere, and their plays have been featured at Dixon Place and Theatre Row in New York City. *Entwined* is their first book. You can connect with Alex on Instagram and TikTok @thatalexalberto, and learn more about their work at alexalberto.com.

Printed in the USA
CPSIA information can be obtained
at www.ICGtesting.com
CBHW020542210124
3570CB00003B/13